Dismantling the Death Penalty

Dismantling the Death Penalty

Research-Based Answers to the Essential Questions

Mark Costanzo, PhD

OXFORD
UNIVERSITY PRESS

OXFORD
UNIVERSITY PRESS

Oxford University Press is a department of the University of Oxford.
It furthers the University's objective of excellence in research, scholarship,
and education by publishing worldwide. Oxford is a registered trade mark of
Oxford University Press in the UK and certain other countries.

Published in the United States of America by Oxford University Press
198 Madison Avenue, New York, NY 10016, United States of America.

CIP data is on file at the Library of Congress

ISBN 978–0–19–751555–6

DOI: 10.1093/oso/9780197515556.001.0001

The manufacturer's authorised representative in the EU for product safety is
Oxford University Press España S.A. of El Parque Empresarial San Fernando
de Henares, Avenida de Castilla, 2 – 28830 Madrid (www.oup.es/en or
product.safety@oup.com). OUP España S.A. also acts as importer into Spain
of products made by the manufacturer.

For Sally, of course

I was in favor of the death penalty, and disposed to regard abolitionists as people whose hearts were bigger than their heads. Four years of close study of the subject gradually dispelled that feeling. In the end I became convinced that the abolitionists were right in their conclusions . . . and that far from the sentimental approach leading into their camp and the rational one into that of the supporters, it was the other way about.

—Sir Ernest Gowers

CONTENTS

NOTE: Because more that 98% of the prisoners on death row are male, masculine pronouns are used throughout this book when referring to capital defendants or condemned prisoners (unless the specific person being discussed is one of the exceedingly rare female or nonbinary defendants or prisoners).

ACKNOWLEDGMENTS

THERE ARE TWO PEOPLE (OTHER than me) who were crucial in bringing this book into print. The first is Sarah Harrington, my editor at Oxford University Press. Sarah's enthusiasm for this project helped sustain me during the long process of writing. She was understanding and supportive when I ran into unexpected delays, and she was always responsive when I had questions or needed advice. I am grateful for her help and expertise.

The other person I am grateful to is Sally Costanzo, my wife. She encouraged me to write this book and provided much needed support along the way. She also edited every page of the book and only asked for nonmonetary compensation. Her knowledge of the topic—she holds a law degree and a PhD—was invaluable in helping me get the facts right. The book is much better because of her efforts.

INTRODUCTION

Why I Wrote This Book

MY BOOKSHELVES HOLD MORE THAN fifty books on the topic of capital punishment. Many of these books are excellent, but most were written primarily for a scholarly audience. *Dismantling the Death Penalty (DDP)* is intended to summarize decades of important, wide-ranging research on capital punishment for a general audience. My goal was to write a clear, engaging book that covers virtually every aspect of the topic. *DDP* has several characteristics which I hope will make it appealing to a broad audience. First, it's a short book. Although the coverage is broad, it is also succinct. Second, the book is organized around questions that naturally arise in the mind of anyone who tries to understand the death penalty in the United States. Third, great care has been taken to present analyses and arguments in a clear, accessible style. Finally, my conclusions about the death penalty are based on the best research currently available. It is my hope that the structure, style, accessibility, and brevity of this book will make it appealing to a broad audience of readers.

The bulk of *DDP* reviews and synthesizes social scientific research on the death penalty. Fortunately, the validity of most claims about the death penalty can be assessed by looking at the research evidence. For example, to determine if executions deter, if the death penalty costs more than life imprisonment, if the public supports executions, and if the penalty is applied without bias or error, we can review the accumulated data. Moreover, even arguments often considered beyond the reach of empirical data—for example, those based on moral and philosophical claims—are considered in this book. Although the emphasis is on social scientific research, case histories (of defendants, trials, and executions) and quotes (from prisoners, lawyers, families of victims, and jurors) are used to illustrate and animate the presentation of research findings.

The opening chapter provides context and foundation for the arguments and evidence that follow. It chronicles the long history of the death penalty and changes in how, when, and why we execute criminals. Chapters 2 through 8 are organized around seven frequently asked questions: How do we decide who is sentenced to death? Does the death penalty deter potential murderers? Does the American public support the death penalty? Is the death penalty "cruel and unusual"? Is the death penalty cheaper than life imprisonment? Are there errors and biases in the application of the death penalty? Is killing murderers morally justified? The closing chapter evaluates the politics and uncertain future of capital punishment.

Dismantling the Death Penalty (DDP) was also written to meet the needs of college students and professors. Many courses—including criminology, criminal justice, psychology and law, introduction to legal studies, contemporary social issues, public policy, and sociology of law—devote significant class time to considering the topic of capital punishment. This thin book can easily be adopted as a supplemental text in such courses, allowing professors the flexibility to assign several other books and articles. And because each chapter of this book is self-contained, professors can also choose to assign only those chapters that are relevant to a particular class.

While writing *DDP*, I often imagined how my students might respond to what I had written. For decades, I have conducted research on the death penalty, and have explored the emotional topic of capital punishment with students in some of my college classes. I have listened to impassioned student discussions and responded to many questions. *DDP* explores all the issues raised by my students. I believe this brief book offers clear, direct, research-based answers to their questions.

I

The Death Penalty from Ancient to Modern Times

A Brief History

KILLING IS AN ANCIENT AND enduring form of punishment. Stoning was one of the earliest forms of execution. These brutal events were often little more than spontaneous eruptions of mob violence. In the Old Testament, Moses offered guidance about the use and purpose of the practice.

> Then shall his father and mother lay hold on him and bring him unto the elders . . . and say this our son is stubborn and rebellious, he will not obey our voice; he is a glutton and a drunkard. And all the men of his city shall stone him with stones, that he die. So shalt thou put evil away from among you; and all Israel shall hear, and fear. (Deut. 21:18–21 [King James Bible, 2017])

Stoning remained a common method of execution for hundreds of years and gradually became, if not more civilized, at least more formal and ritualized. Among the ancient Greeks and Hebrews, an etiquette of execution began to emerge. All that was necessary to trigger a stoning was an accusation by two witnesses with good standing in the community. Accusers would place their hands on the head of the defendant and describe the crime they had witnessed. The doomed person was then walked, carried, or dragged to a tall rock or an elevated scaffold. With hands tied, the convict was stripped naked and then pushed from the platform by one of the witnesses. The second witness had the honor of casting the first stone. If the condemned person still showed signs of life, the people gathered to watch the execution joined in until the victim's bloody body lay motionless beneath a pile of rocks (Johnson, 1990).

Other forms of execution were soon devised. *Lingchi*—also known as "death by a thousand cuts"—was used in imperial China and remained in use until 1905. The technique produced an excruciating death by the slow carving away of small bits of flesh over a period of hours (Brook et al., 2008). During the rule of the Rajahs in nineteenth-century India, elephants were sometimes used to make executions especially terrifying and excruciating.

> The culprit, bound hand and foot, is fastened by a long cord, passed round his waist, to the elephant's hind leg. The latter is urged into a rapid trot through the streets of the city, and every step gives the cord a violent jerk, which makes the body of the condemned wretch pound on the pavement. . . . Then his head is placed upon a stone, and the elephant executioner crushes it beneath his enormous foot. (Andersen, 1983)

In England, from as early as 1241 to as late as 1820, those convicted of capital crimes were hanged, drawn, and quartered. The prisoner was taken from his prison cell and laid on a sledge, which was tied to a horse and dragged along the ground to the gallows. At the gallows, the prisoner slowly strangled while dangling from a rope (the "long drop," which snaps the spinal cord, was a modern innovation in hanging). The executioner was often instructed to cut down the prisoner when "half dead," at which point the convict was disemboweled, his entrails thrown into a nearby fire, his head cut off, and his body cut into quarters (Andrews, 1991). The decapitation and "quartering" of the transgressor served both dramatic and practical ends: It added power to the execution ceremony and provided five parts of the corpse that could be displayed at conspicuous sites as visible warnings to potential wrongdoers. Indeed, during the seventeenth and eighteenth centuries, several major crossroads in London were decorated with decaying corpses hanging from trees or stuck on poles. London Bridge was adorned with the heads of the recently executed, such heads having been "parboiled" (cooked in salt and cumin seed) to delay the decaying process and render them unappetizing to birds. Judging from an account in 1665, this process was apparently quite effective.

And here I cannot omit to declare unto you the miraculous sight of this head, which,   after it had stood up the space of fourteen days upon the bridge, could not be perceived to waste nor consume; . . . but grew daily fresher and fresher, so that in his lifetime he never looked so well; for his cheeks being beautified with a comely red, the face looked as though it had beholden the people passing by, and would have spoken to them. (quoted in Abbott, 1991)

Stoning and hanging were not the only methods of execution in early times—only the most common. An impressive amount of sadistic creativity went into devising methods for killing those who dared to break the law. Some techniques involved little preparation or equipment: throwing the offender into a quagmire to drown; beating to death with fists, feet, and sticks; and beheading by sword or ax. More elaborate forms of execution included "breaking on the wheel" (popular in eighteenth-century Germany and France) and "pressing to death." The "wheel" involved binding the hands and feet of the criminal to a large cartwheel. The wheel was positioned on an incline with the criminal facing outward to afford a better view of the spectacle. It was important for the audience to have a clear view because public officials believed that witnessing these gruesome executions would inspire fear and keep others from breaking the law. The executioner, wielding an iron bar, methodically broke the arms and legs in several places before bringing death by a blow to the throat or the heart. The procedure might involve as many as forty blows and last as long as two hours (Scott, 1950).

"Pressing" took longer and was generally reserved for those who were reluctant to confess to crimes they may or may not have committed. The prisoner was stripped naked and tied, faceup, to the floor of the prison cell while iron or stone weights were loaded on him. More weights were piled on over hours or days, producing agony but not death. The execution procedure required that the prisoner "shall have no more sustenance but the worst bread and water," and that "he shall not eat the same day on which he drinks, nor drink the same day on which he eats; and he shall so continue until he dies" (Andrews, 1991, p. 204). Not surprisingly, this procedure was almost always successful in extracting the desired confession. Following the confession, the pressing could continue until the prisoner died.

For more than a century, capital punishment was not confined to humans. In several European countries, animals who killed humans might also find their way to the gallows. Of course, pigs, cows, and horses could not provide useful testimony on their own behalf, but humans could provide eyewitness or character testimony. Attorneys defended animals accused of murder in trials quite similar to those afforded human defendants. In 1396, a pig accused of fatally injuring a child was dressed in the suit of a man and publicly hanged (Scott, 1950). In 1750, a man and a donkey accused of having sexual intercourse were scheduled to be burned together at the stake. In the end, the donkey was spared because a local priest and other leading citizens testified that the beast was of noble character and an unwilling participant in the depravity. The man, however, was not so lucky (Evans, 1906).

Method and style of execution depended not only on the gravity of the crime, but also on the gender and social standing of the offender. Burning at the stake was typically reserved for women. Though burning is surely a hideous way to die, it was considered far less excruciating than the disemboweling and quartering men faced for similar crimes. A woman who was tarred and bound before the fire was lit could be "mercifully" strangled at the stake before the flames enveloped her body. There was also the question of decorum. As Sir William Blackstone explained, women were granted the more dignified method of death because "the decency due to their sex forbids exposing and publicly mangling their bodies" (Horwitz, 1973). Blackstone adds that such small kindnesses reveal the "humanity of the English nation." In England, one final accommodation was made to women: pregnancy could postpone or prevent execution. If the condemned was known to be or suspected of being pregnant, a panel of twelve matrons was appointed to investigate the matter further. If the panel determined that the prisoner was with child, a stay was granted. But mercy had its limits—many women were hanged shortly after giving birth in their prison cell. In 1931, a law was passed forbidding the death sentence for pregnant women.

In France, the guillotine was introduced in 1792 and remained in use for more than a century. The machine was touted as a modern and merciful method of killing. It was considered a humane alternative to beheading by sword or axe, which were heavily dependent on the skill of the executioner and the sharpness of the blade. The weighted blade of the guillotine was able to swiftly separate heads from the bodies of the condemned. However, even this less gruesome spectacle was not free of blood.

When the blade cuts through the neck of the condemned one, three unequal jets spurt out forcefully: the two carotids project blood in powerful jets that can exceed two meters; in the center there is a lesser whitish jet extending 30 centimeters, namely the cerebrospinal fluid that, brutally compressed, spurts from the severed vertebral column. The receptacle that the head falls into has an external wall high enough to stop these spurts of blood. But there is some splashing, clumsiness. One inconvenience of the job of the executioner is that his clothes are soiled. (cited in Wills, 2019, p. 87)

Executions in the United States

More than four centuries have passed since the first documented lawful execution on American soil in 1608 (Captain George Kendall was killed by firing squad in Virginia for the crime of espionage; Schneider & Smykla, 1991). Although early colonial laws were adapted from British law, capital punishment in the colonies was both more humane and more restricted than in seventeenth-century England. At a time when drawing and quartering, disemboweling, and burning at the stake were still commonplace in the civilized countries of Europe, hanging—at the time regarded as the most humane method—was almost always the means of execution in the colonies. However, just as in Europe, executions were festive public spectacles. The condemned was forced to take a slow wagon ride to the gallows, sometimes sitting atop the very coffin he or she would soon occupy. The rowdy crowds who witnessed the hangings often numbered in the thousands.

Under British law at the time, there were more than fifty capital offenses (including vagrancy, heresy, witchcraft, rape, murder, and treason) while, on average, only about a dozen crimes were punishable by death in the colonies (Hook & Kahn, 1989). But lists of capital crimes varied widely by territory. Puritan-influenced Massachusetts Bay Colony listed statutory rape, rebellion, adultery, buggery, idolatry, witchcraft, bestiality, man-stealing, and blasphemy as capital crimes. In contrast, Quaker-influenced South Jersey declined to adopt capital punishment in its original charter. Behaviors that threatened property or the social-economic order were often designated as capital crimes. In North Carolina, for example, capital offenses included circulating seditious literature among slaves, inciting slaves to insurrection, slave stealing, and harboring slaves for the purpose of setting them free. Similarly, Virginia listed only five capital crimes for White people, but seventy for Black people (Bedau, 1982).

Lynching, an unofficial form of execution, was widespread in early America and used extensively against Black men. Those who were frustrated with the workings of the legal system often formed spontaneous mobs of vigilantes. Although records are sparse, it appears that the number of lynchings in America peaked during the 1890s, at about 1,540. This exceeded the number of state-authorized executions by 442 during the same period (Bowers et al., 1984).

The Abolition Movement

The movement to abolish the death penalty in America has been marked by a long series of advances and retreats. In 1787, at the home of Benjamin Franklin, influential citizens of Philadelphia gathered to hear an eloquent speech by Benjamin Rush, a physician and signer of the Declaration of Independence. Rush, whose thinking was indebted to the Italian Enlightenment thinker and jurist Cesare Beccaria, argued that executions brutalized the population and were an improper use of state power. Rush's efforts gave momentum to the abolition movement, and, by 1793, Pennsylvania's attorney general, William Bradford, proposed the notion of *degrees* of murder. Bradford defined first-degree murder as "willful, deliberate, and premeditated killing" or murder committed during "arson, rape, robbery, or burglary." His distinction was formally adopted the following year and use of the death penalty became restricted to first-degree murder. Pennsylvania also launched a national trend in 1834 by banning public executions. Although public executions were quite rare after the dawn of the twentieth century, public interest in such spectacles had not waned. In 1936, the last American public hanging (in Kentucky) attracted a crowd of nearly twenty thousand (Horwitz, 1973).

In 1838, Tennessee abandoned mandatory death sentences for capital crimes and gave jurors the option of imposing a sentence other than death. A few states went even farther. Michigan eliminated capital punishment for all crimes except treason in 1846, twenty years earlier than any European nation. Rhode Island and Wisconsin became the first two states to eliminate capital punishment for all crimes in 1852 and 1853, respectively (Bedau, 1982). At least until the early 1900s, the abolitionist movement appeared to be gathering momentum. But some states that experimented with abolition later reinstated the death penalty (e.g., Kansas). Other states have abolished the penalty, then reinstated it, and later abolished it again (e.g., Colorado). At present, twenty-four states, the US military, and the federal government authorize capital punishment. States without the death penalty include Alaska, Colorado, Connecticut, Delaware, Hawaii, Illinois, Iowa, Maine, Maryland, Massachusetts, Michigan, Minnesota, New Hampshire, New Jersey, New Mexico, New York, North Dakota, Rhode Island, Vermont, Virginia, Washington, West Virginia, and Wisconsin. Three states—California, Oregon, and Pennsylvania—have moratoria on executions.

The number of death sentences and executions in the United States has always been small when compared to the number of murders. People convicted of murder are rarely sentenced to death and are even more rarely executed. The rate of execution peaked in 1938, when there were 2.01 executions per 100 homicides in states with the death penalty. The annual number of executions reached a record high in 1935, when 199 people were put to death. Following the 1930s, the number of executions declined steadily for about thirty years until executions halted for nearly a decade. The future of capital punishment appeared to be tenuous. By the late 1960s, public support for capital punishment had dropped to historic lows, and there were no executions in the United States for three years in a row. By 1970, the Supreme Court announced that it would hear a case that had the potential to abolish capital punishment nationally. Because of the anticipation of that ruling and the aftermath of the subsequent landmark ruling, there were no executions between June 3, 1967, and January 17, 1977.

In 1972, the Supreme Court evaluated the constitutionality of the death penalty in the case of *Furman v. Georgia*. Evidence of "arbitrary and discriminatory" sentencing persuaded the Court that the death penalty, as then administered, violated the Eighth Amendment's prohibition against "cruel and unusual punishment." However, a few years later, in *Gregg v. Georgia* (1976) and its companion cases, the Court decided that, by restructuring the capital trial and guiding the discretion of jurors, death sentences could be applied fairly (Costanzo & Costanzo, 1992). The moratorium on executions ended in 1977, when convicted murderer Gary Gilmore halted further appeals on his behalf and demanded to be killed by a Utah firing squad. Since Gilmore's execution, more than 1,500 people have been executed. Nearly 60% of these executions have taken place in just four southern states: Texas, Virginia, Oklahoma, and Florida. Texas alone has carried out more than 37% of all executions in the United States since 1976. Virginia carried out the second most executions during that time span, but, in 2021, it abolished its death penalty.

When researchers make lists of countries that have abolished or retained the death penalty, the United States is always placed in the retentionist column. In one sense, that's a fair classification. But it is important to keep in mind that whether to allow or prohibit the death penalty has largely been a state-by-state decision. And nearly half the states have already decided to abolish the penalty. Unlike most other countries, the United States does not have one unified system of capital punishment. Instead, there are currently twenty-six mostly separate systems (twenty-four in states with the death penalty, plus the military and federal systems). Although the US Supreme Court could again decide that capital punishment is unconstitutional and thereby abolish it nationwide, so far, the road to abolition has run through the states.

For more than two decades, researchers and legal scholars have been predicting the death of the death penalty in the United States. The numbers support that prediction. Between 2000 and 2023, fifteen states either abolished capital punishment or began governor-initiated moratoria. The number of death sentences and executions also showed a strong downward trend. From 2001 through 2010, 1,349 defendants were convicted and sentenced to death and 551 prisoners were executed. From 2011 through 2020, 536 defendants were convicted and sentenced to death, and 295 prisoners were executed. The many reasons for these steep declines are discussed in the chapters that follow.

Justifications for Killing Criminals

In ancient times, one murder would often incite several other murders and fuel an expanding "blood feud." A victim's family might seek vengeance by killing a member of the murderer's family, provoking an expanding cycle of murder and retaliation. By seizing control over the punishment of murderers, the state preserved community order and restricted the scope of killing. A murder was avenged by taking only the life of the murderer, and the nearest relative of the victim was sometimes permitted to serve as judge and executioner. This method of satisfying the urge for revenge helped to maintain social order and prevented blood feuds from spinning out of control.

Capital punishment was not the only penalty for murder. For example, the Anglo-Saxons developed an elaborate system of fines. Instead of killing the murderer, a payment to the family of the victim could sometimes be substituted, with the assessed fine depending on the official value of the victim's life: "If a freeman slew his thrall, he paied a nominal fine to the king for a breach of the peace; but if a slave killed his master the doctrine of blood for blood was carried into effect" (Scott, 1950, p. 5).

Early justifications for killing wrongdoers usually rested on religious authority. Religious leaders insisted that executions were a means of carrying out the will of God. According to the laws of Moses, the death penalty was a way to appease God and avert famines, plagues, and other misfortunes that might result from "God's fierce anger" against any community that failed to punish sinners. The sinner was killed to "purge the evil from the midst of you" (Deut. 17:7 [King James Bible, 2017]).

In New England, the religious nature of the execution was made explicit by the practice of having ministers deliver a sermon from the gallows as a prelude to a hanging. These sermons, which were delivered routinely from 1674 to as late as 1825, relied heavily upon Scripture and emphasized the community's duty to avenge God and avoid his wrath. Spectators were warned that, "if we will not pronounce such a villain accursed, we must be content to bear the curse ourselves. . . . The land cannot be cleansed, until it hath spued out this unclean beast" (Cohen, 1988, p. 150). As American society became more secular, scriptural justifications began to lose some of their resonance. Simple vengeance then rose to become the dominant justification. Vengeance served as a compelling justification for several decades, until religious and political leaders began to challenge the morality of revenge.

Justifications for the death penalty rested not only on divine law but also on human order. Noah Hobart, a leading Connecticut minister, argued in 1768 that the goal of punishment was peace and security and that the seriousness of a crime is measured by the "tendency to destroy the public good, or the safety and happiness of society" (Cohen, 1988, p. 154). The moral authority of the state was highlighted by emphasizing the fairness of the legal procedures that led to conviction and execution. By 1800, gallows sermons reminded audiences that the condemned prisoner, "had the assistance of the most able counsellors and advocates, who appeared to adduce every argument and motive that might possibly operate in his favor." Further, the prisoner was reminded that "the evidence was so clear against you as to induce twelve sober, judicious, disinterested jurors, on their oath to pronounce you guilty" (Cohen, 1988, p. 158).

Deterrence, with its considerable intuitive appeal, has always been the most prominent element of arguments seeking to justify capital punishment based on social benefits. According to the deterrence argument, the death penalty actually saves lives by discouraging potential murderers. The Greek philosopher Pythagoras expressed faith in the principle of deterrence, and the Roman philosopher Seneca argued that "the more public the punishments are, the greater the effect they will produce upon the reformation of others" (Laurence, 1931, p. 4). English thinkers such as William Paley helped shape the American colonists' view of the utility of punishment. In 1790, Paley wrote that the aim of punishment was not revenge but "prevention against future offenses of the same kind . . . by deterring others by the dread of his example" (Paley, 1790, p. 12). The theory of deterrence remains a major justification even today.

Leaving aside the validity of the theory of deterrence for the moment (it is the subject of Chapter 3), its ascendance poses a fundamental problem: If punishment deters, then harsh punishments should deter best, and the very best results should be obtained if many types of crimes are punished in the harshest possible manner. If the penalty of death deters murder, then it should also deter theft or adultery or blasphemy. And if the possibility of death isn't a powerful enough deterrent, death could be made more terrifying by torturing before execution and dismembering the corpse after death. As noted by one historian, "No means was deemed too foul, too savage, or too inhuman, if it were thought to prove an effective deterrent" (Scott, 1950, p. 8). Today, while justifications based on divine law and deterrence persist, their relative importance has faded. Other rationales for support or opposition have moved to the foreground: financial cost, public support, cruelty, fairness of application, racial discrimination, and wrongful conviction. These issues are closely examined in the chapters that follow.

Five Historical Trends

The death penalty has evolved over centuries. If we look carefully at this long evolution, we can spot five consistent trends. The first trend has been a dramatic shrinking in the number and types of crimes punishable by death. For some 150 years in England (until 1820), more than 200 crimes were punishable by death. Petty theft and other crimes that seem trivial by modern standards could cost a criminal his or her life. As one observer put it, "We hanged for everything—for a shilling— for five shillings—for witchcraft—for things that were and things that could not be" (Cooper, 1974, p. 27). In most countries, the list of capital crimes kept shrinking until the death penalty itself was finally erased from the law of the land. The renowned attorney Anthony Amsterdam saw this trend as "the slow but absolutely certain progress of maturing civilizations that will bring an inevitable end to punishment by death" (Amsterdam, 1982, p. 347). In most countries this "inevitable end" has already been reached. The United States now stands alone as the only Western democracy that still executes its own citizens.

Even in the United States, lists of capital crimes have been steadily shortened so that, in most states, the list now includes only first-degree murder with "special circumstances." Circumstances that define a murder as "death eligible" vary from state to state but generally include the following: (1) murder committed in the commission of a felony (e.g., robbery, rape, or kidnapping); (2) multiple murder; (3) murder of a police or correctional officer acting in the line of duty; (4) especially cruel or heinous murder; (5) murder for financial gain; (6) murder by an offender having a prior conviction for a violent crime; and (7) causing or directing another to commit murder. Most capital cases involve defendants charged with the first circumstance—murder during the commission of a felony (so-called felony-murder). Military and federal law authorize the death penalty for murder, but also for crimes involving terrorism, treason, espionage, and sedition.

A second trend is the narrowing of who is eligible for the death penalty. In the *Atkins v. Virginia* decision in 2002, the US Supreme Court put an end to the practice of executing prisoners with very limited intellectual capacities. The ruling held that "a national consensus" had developed against executing intellectually disabled prisoners and that "because of their disabilities in the areas of reasoning, judgment, and control of their impulses . . . they do not act with the level of moral culpability that characterizes the most serious adult criminal conduct." Three years later, in *Roper v. Simmons* (2005), the Court abolished the death penalty for juvenile offenders. The justices based their ruling, in part, on research in cognitive neuroscience indicating that key psychological capacities—such as impulse control, rational decision-making, and long-term foresight—are not yet fully developed in juveniles. The Court reasoned that people who committed capital murder before the age of eighteen should not be executed because they are inherently less culpable for their crimes.

A third trend involves the attempt to lessen the cruelty of executions by replacing one execution technology with another, seemingly more humane, technology. Without exception, the claim has been that each new method was quicker, less painful, and less barbaric than its predecessor. For example, in 1792, Dr. Guillotin optimistically declared that the victims of his killing device would feel nothing more than a "slight sensation of coldness on the neck." In a similar vein, former President Ronald Reagan used a folksy analogy to suggest that lethal injection might produce a quick, painless death for condemned prisoners.

> I know what it's like to try to eliminate an injured horse by shooting him. Now you call the veterinarian, and he gives it a shot and the horse goes to sleep—that's it. I myself have wondered . . . if there aren't even more humane methods now—the simple shot or tranquillizer. (Zimring & Hawkins, 1986, p. 110)

In the 1800s, hanging was the most common means of execution. It was eventually replaced by electrocution, then by lethal gas, and, most recently, by lethal injection. Currently, all states that retain capital punishment, as well as the military and the federal government, use lethal injection as their sole or primary means of killing. In the few states that authorize more than one method, the condemned prisoner is usually able to choose an alternative authorized method (e.g., electrocution, firing squad, or lethal gas). Although each change in the method of killing was designed to make executions more humane, questions have been raised about the purported "humaneness" of every method. Because some states are considering a return to older methods (the firing squad) and other states are considering new, untested methods (nitrogen hypoxia), issues of humaneness will remain prominent. The question of whether the death penalty is "cruel and unusual" is central to the debate and will be examined at length in Chapter 5.

A fourth trend has been the attempt by policymakers to ensure that death sentences are imposed fairly and rationally. In an effort to make imposition of the death penalty fair, courts and legislatures have, at various times, enacted mandatory death sentences for specified crimes, forbidden the practice of mandatory death sentences, broadened the sentencing discretion of jurors, and narrowed the sentencing discretion of jurors. Unfortunately, these efforts have failed to produce a fair and rational system of capital punishment. This issue of fairness will be discussed in Chapter 7. Race, wealth, and even geography continue to influence which defendants are sentenced to live out their lives in prison and which are sentenced to die in the execution chamber.

The fifth trend involves what might be called the sanitizing of executions. In the 1700s and early 1800s, executions were often public events witnessed by hundreds or thousands of rowdy spectators. A carnival atmosphere prevailed, and the day's festivities often included several hangings. Execution was swift, often occurring only days or weeks after conviction. In contrast, today's executions occur inside prisons, using well-specified, bureaucratic procedures. These modern events are witnessed by only a handful of observers (e.g., journalists, relatives of the condemned prisoner, relatives of the victim) and occur, on average, about sixteen years after conviction (DPIC, 2023). Unfortunately, the well-intentioned regulation of our system of capital punishment (and even the use of such euphemisms as "capital punishment") has the secondary effect of enabling citizens to distance themselves psychologically from the act of killing. Albert Camus made the point forcefully more than sixty years ago.

> The survival of such a primitive rite has been made possible only by the thoughtlessness or ignorance of the public. . . . When the imagination sleeps, words are emptied of their meaning: a deaf population absent-mindedly registers the condemnation of a man. But if people are shown the machine, made to touch the wood and steel and to hear the sound of a head falling, then public imagination, suddenly awakened, will repudiate both the vocabulary and the penalty. (Camus, 1960, p. 18)

In our time, the public imagination still sleeps, but it is an uneasy, fitful sleep. The crushing costs and troubling consequences of the death penalty have become increasingly hard to ignore. This book is an attempt not only to "show the machine," but also to expose the social, political, moral, and economic consequences of killing people who have killed.

2

How Do We Decide Who Is Sentenced to Death?

IMAGINE THAT YOU ARE A juror in a capital murder trial. You have just convicted a man of first-degree murder with special circumstances. You and eleven other jurors must now decide whether he should live out his life in prison or die by execution. What information would you need to have at your disposal? What issues would you need to consider? What would convince you that someone deserves to be killed for his crimes? What might make you decide to show mercy, to send the man to a life in prison instead of the execution chamber?

How jurors decide which defendants should die has been a pivotal issue in Supreme Court rulings for more than half a century. Justices and legislators have tinkered with both trial procedures and jury instructions in an effort to correct problems with capital sentencing. The challenge is to fashion a process that minimizes arbitrary sentencing decisions based on legally irrelevant criteria (e.g., race, wealth, gender) while simultaneously allowing jurors to consider the unique circumstances of each case. The issue confronting the Court has been whether this delicate balance can be achieved in practice, whether death sentencing can be both fair and rational.

Many have doubted the capacity of the courts to regulate the nature and scope of penalty decision-making. As Justice John Harlan wrote more than fifty years ago,

To identify before the fact those characteristics of criminal homicides and their perpetrators which call for the death penalty, and to express these characteristics in language which can be fairly understood and applied by the sentencing authority, appear to be tasks which are beyond present human ability. (*McGautha v. California*, 1971, p. 402)

Just prior to his retirement, Justice Blackmun came to share Justice Harlan's view. In *Callins v. Collins* (1994), Blackmun declared that his support for the death penalty had come to an end. "From this day forward, I no longer shall tinker with the machinery of death," he wrote in an eloquent dissent. After struggling for more than twenty years "to develop procedural and substantive rules that would lend more than the mere appearance of fairness to the death penalty endeavor," he reached the conclusion that our system of capital punishment still "fails to deliver the fair, consistent, and reliable sentences of death required by the Constitution."

Two Supreme Court Decisions

Before a prisoner is killed in the execution chamber, there has been a period of confinement on death row, and there may have been a variety of appeals. Most important, there has been a capital murder trial that culminated in a guilty verdict and sentence of death. The process begins when the defendant enters a courtroom and ends when a corpse is carried from the execution chamber.

Until the early 1970s, juries were given broad discretion in making the life-or-death sentencing decision. Then, in 1972, everything changed. In the landmark case *Furman v. Georgia*, the Supreme Court ruled that capital punishment—as then administered—was unconstitutional. Two constitutional questions were at issue: the Eighth Amendment's prohibition against "cruel and unusual punishment" and the Fourteenth Amendment's guarantee of "equal protection" under the law. The *Furman* decision overturned more than 600 death sentences and, primarily because of *Furman*, there was a nationwide moratorium on executions that began in 1967 and lasted nearly a decade.

In *Furman*, Stanford law professor Anthony Amsterdam blended legal theory with social science to wage a devastating assault on the death penalty. His presentation before the Court—one justice later described it as the best he had ever heard—consisted of four arguments (Woodward & Armstrong, 1979). First, he presented overwhelming statistical evidence that African Americans and poor defendants were far more likely to receive death sentences. Nine out of every ten people executed for rape had been Black, and more than half the prisoners executed since 1930 had been Black. A second argument was that the death penalty was imposed in an inconsistent and arbitrary manner: Armed robbery might send a man to the electric chair while murder might lead to a thirty-year prison sentence. The death penalty resembled a lethal lottery. Third, it was argued that because the death penalty was so rarely imposed, it could not be defended as an effective deterrent to crime. From 1960 to 1964, the average number of executions was thirty-six per year. The national count fell sharply after that: seven in 1965, one in 1966, two in 1967, and none at all between 1968 and 1972. The fourth and final argument was that societal standards of decency had evolved beyond the practice of killing as a form of punishment.

After hearing these compelling arguments, two of the justices, Thurgood Marshall and William Brennan, were ready to abolish the death penalty for good. Three other justices—Potter Stewart, Byron White, and William O. Douglas—joined with Brennan and Marshall to form a decisive majority. Justice Stewart concluded that the death penalty was "wantonly and freakishly applied," and Justice White observed that "there is no meaningful basis for distinguishing the few cases in which it is imposed from the many cases in which it is not." Justice Douglas pointed to "the uncontrolled discretion of judges or juries" and concluded that "no standards govern selection of the penalty." The existing system of capital punishment was thus ruled unconstitutional in a 5-to-4 decision. Justice Stewart told his clerks that "The death penalty in America was finished," and Justice Burger told his clerks, "There will never be another execution in the country" (Mandery, 2013, p. 242).

It was a resounding victory for abolitionists, but not an enduring one. Although five of the justices had voted to strike down the death penalty, the reasoning underlying their votes differed markedly. The deeply contentious decision splintered the Court. Nine separate opinions were issued, and, at more than 50,000 words, *Furman* stands as the lengthiest—and one of the most passionate—Supreme Court decisions ever made. Most important, although the *Furman* majority condemned the "arbitrary and discriminatory" pattern of death sentences, it did not prohibit use of the death penalty in principle. It was merely the *current administration* of capital punishment that was prohibited.

Especially in southern states, politicians were infuriated by the *Furman* decision. Not only did the public want the death penalty restored, but state legislators also resented the restriction of state authority by the federal government. Those legislators labored long and hard to find ways of making capital punishment constitutional again. By reworking death penalty sentencing procedures, they hoped to ease the concerns of the Court. By 1976, the Court was ready to review several of the modified sentencing schemes. And, by that time, a crucial Justice—William O. Douglas—had retired and been replaced by the more conservative John Paul Stevens. Two of the Justices in the *Furman* majority, Potter Stewart and Byron White, seemed ready to reverse their earlier votes. The stage was set for another divisive fight over the constitutionality of the death penalty.

Two basic sentencing schemes were submitted by the states. North Carolina (*Woodson v. North Carolina*, 1976) and Louisiana (*Roberts v. Louisiana*, 1976) proposed mandatory death sentences for certain types of murder, thereby erasing all discretion. The reasoning was that arbitrariness and discrimination could be eliminated if there was no room for any discretion. But the facts in *Woodson* highlighted the need to take into account the unique characteristics of each case. James Woodson had waited in a getaway car while his two accomplices robbed a convenience store, killing the clerk and wounding a customer. One of the accomplices traded his testimony for a twenty-year sentence, and Woodson received an automatic death sentence for his participation. Clearly, automatic sentencing had not corrected the type of inequities that led the Court to strike down capital punishment four years earlier.

The Supreme Court rejected automatic death sentences by a 5-to-4 majority. The majority argued that mandatory death sentences offended the "evolving standards of decency" referred to in *Furman* and that such laws permitted very different cases to be treated as though they were identical. According to the majority, consistent application of the penalty was essential because "the penalty of death is qualitatively different from a sentence of imprisonment, however long." The majority further explained that "[automatic death sentencing] does not fulfill *Furman's* basic requirement by replacing arbitrary and wanton jury discretion with objective standards to guide, regularize, and make rationally reviewable the process for imposing a sentence of death" (*Woodson v. North Carolina*, 1976, p. 303).

Georgia, Texas, and Florida proposed a "non-automatic" alternative scheme that attempted to restrain and guide juror discretion during the sentencing decision. This "guided discretion" protocol eased the concerns of the Court and was ultimately approved by a plurality of the justices. In *Furman*, the justices had laid the blame for arbitrary application on the "unfettered discretion" afforded jurors. In *Gregg v. Georgia*, the Court approved a series of reforms intended to eliminate arbitrary and discriminatory death sentences. Under these new "guided discretion" statutes, only certain types of murder (first-degree murder with special circumstances) were eligible for the death penalty. Defendants accused of capital murder would be tried by jury in a two-phase proceeding. Guilt would be assessed in the first phase, and, if the defendant was found guilty of a capital crime, sentence would be decided by the same jury in the second, "penalty" phase (sometimes called the "sentencing" phase). In the penalty trial, the jury would answer a single profound question: Should the defendant be sentenced to life imprisonment or death by execution? Finally, to further assure impartial application of the penalty, death verdicts would be automatically reviewed by state supreme courts.

With these reforms in place, the majority was confident that the problems cited in *Furman* would be eliminated. "It seems clear . . . that the problem will be alleviated if the jury is given guidance regarding the factors about the crime and the defendant that the State, representing organized society, deems particularly relevant to the sentencing decision" (*Gregg v. Georgia*, 1976, p. 195). The majority seemed to share the belief that "the issues posed in the sentencing proceeding have a common-sense core of meaning and that criminal juries should be capable of understanding them" (*Gregg v. Georgia*, 1976, p. 192).

In its quest for fairness, the Court focused its attention on the sentencing decision-maker: the jury. The jury is told to follow guidelines intended to restrain its discretion. Jurors must consider both the crime and the mitigating circumstances presented in the unique biography of the defendant. The new view of the Court was that guided discretion and appellate review were the key components of a constitutional death penalty. As a result of *Gregg*, death sentences were revived. Executions resumed in 1977, when Gary Gilmore—who had halted further appeals on his behalf—was shot and killed by a Utah firing squad. His famous last words to the four men who aimed their rifles at his heart were, "Let's do it."

In the decades following the *Gregg* decision, the Supreme Court attempted to refine the penalty-phase proceedings. *Lockett v. Ohio* (1978) held that the sentencer must "not be precluded from considering, as a mitigating factor, any aspect of a defendant's character or record and any of the circumstances of the offense that the defendant proffers as a basis for a sentence less than death" (p. 604). *Eddings v. Oklahoma* (1984) ruled that while jurors "may determine the weight to be given to relevant mitigating evidence," they "may not give it no weight by excluding such evidence from consideration" (p. 114). *Barclay v. Florida* (1983) held that the jury may consider aggravating circumstances not mentioned in the relevant statute, and *Skipper v. South Carolina* (1986) held that evidence pertaining to the defendant's future behavior and potential adjustment to prison could be relevant sentencing considerations. In *California v. Brown* (1987), it was ruled constitutional to instruct the jury not to be influenced by "mere sympathy," and *Payne v. Tennessee* (1991) held that jurors could consider the harm that the victim's death caused his or her survivors.

In general, in a series of decisions after *Gregg*, the high Court signaled that it will "no longer regulate what a penalty jury hears, except to approve the procedures by which the jury gets to hear as much as possible" (Weisburg, 1994, p. 344). In *Ring v. Arizona* (2002), the Court held that, before a death penalty can be imposed, a jury (not just a judge) must find that one or more aggravating factors was present beyond a reasonable doubt. In 2016, extending the reasoning used in *Ring*, the Court ruled that Florida's capital sentencing procedure violated the Sixth Amendment's guarantee of a right to trial by jury (*Hurst v. Florida*, 2016). Florida law treated a jury's sentence as merely "advisory," which meant that a judge could impose a sentence of death even if the jury had decided on life without parole (LWOP). The Court held that a death sentence must be based "on a jury's verdict, not a judge's fact-finding."

The Bifurcated Capital Murder Trial

The road to the execution chamber begins with the capital murder trial. The two-phase structure of the capital trial is unique in our justice system. The first phase, referred to as the "guilt" phase, is similar to other types of criminal trials. Using the available evidence, prosecutors must prove beyond a reasonable doubt that the defendant committed the murder. But, unlike other criminal trials, if the jury finds the defendant guilty of capital murder, a second, "penalty" phase begins. In the penalty phase, jurors must decide whether the defendant should be killed in the execution chamber.

Jurors play a uniquely prominent role in capital trials. In most criminal cases, jurors decide only whether a defendant is guilty. Decisions about punishment, if necessary, are left to the judge, who has a better understanding of various sentencing options (e.g., incarceration, probation, diversion programs) and their availability for a given defendant. But in capital cases, these concerns are moot. The penalty phase is qualitatively different from all other types of trials because the question posed to jurors is not, "What happened?" but, instead, "Does this defendant deserve to be killed or spared?" Conventional forms of evidence and the usual standards of proof no longer apply. The judge is no more qualified than the jury to make such a profound moral choice. Indeed, the jury is believed to be better equipped to make this decision, and it is hoped that the jury will reflect the conscience and values of the larger community. Yet, although a particular jury may provide a crude approximation of societal values, its members rarely possess experience in sentencing decisions or even clearly defined notions of who deserves the death penalty and who does not. In the penalty phase, jurors hear testimony about "aggravating" factors (that can be used to support a sentence of death) and "mitigating" factors (that can be used to support a sentence of life imprisonment). Juries are permitted to sentence the defendant to death if aggravating factors outweigh mitigating factors.

Whereas most trials focus on logic and evidence, the penalty phase focuses on the defendant's motivation, character, and life history. Moving beyond facts and evidence, defenders and prosecutors give reasons for the actions of the defendant, explore the consequences of the murder, and show how the recommended sentence is consistent with widely held moral principles. Defense attorneys must try to humanize their client by presenting a plausible explanation for the defendant's despicable behavior. If jurors are to show mercy, they must be able to see the murderer as a human being, not merely as a one-dimensional, remorseless monster whose actions are beyond understanding. This humanizing of the defendant is typically accomplished by placing his violent conduct in a larger context. Brothers, sisters, parents, children, neighbors, teachers, friends, and co-workers may testify about the defendant's character and life. In a well-conducted penalty phase, the life story of the defendant is painstakingly reconstructed so that the jurors who will decide his fate can understand the events and influences that contributed to his murderous behavior. One psychological expert describes the difficulty of the task in this way:

The range of factors that impact developmental trajectory and adult functioning are extraordinarily broad. Accordingly, a mental health expert addressing mitigation and moral culpability at capital sentencing faces the daunting task of identifying any factors that might adversely impact physical, neuropsychological, psychoeducational, personality, social/interpersonal, moral, and vocational development and capabilities. (Cunningham, 2016, p. 211)

The Impact of "Death Qualification" on Capital Juries

Potential capital jurors are randomly selected from a large jury pool. Prosecuting attorneys, defense attorneys, and the judge then ask potential jurors a series of questions to determine who will serve on the jury. This process is known as *voir dire* (French for "to say the truth"). As a result of the *voir dire* process, most potential jurors are eventually excused from service. Attorneys are permitted to excuse jurors from service through "challenges for cause" or through "peremptory challenges." In a challenge for cause, an attorney will claim that a juror's answers indicate that he or she is unable to be fair and impartial or is unable to follow the law (e.g., a juror might say that she would hold it against a defendant if he chose not to testify on his own behalf). There is no limit on the number of challenges for cause. Attorneys can also oust a juror by using one of a limited number of peremptory challenges (challenges for which no reason need be stated). What is usually referred to as "jury selection" is actually a process of deselection: Each jury is made up of people who were not successfully challenged by either the prosecution or the defense.

The process just described is like the process of assembling a jury for any other type of criminal trial. But in a capital case, *voir dire* includes the added procedure of "death qualification." The process of death qualification is unique to capital trials. In addition to routine questions about attitudes and personal experiences thought to be pertinent to the case, prospective capital jurors are asked if they will be able to consider a death sentence if the defendant is found guilty of a capital crime. In 1985, the US Supreme Court ruled that potential jurors whose beliefs "substantially impair" their ability to impose a death sentence must be excused from serving on a capital jury (*Wainwright v. Witt*, 1985). Thus, if a potential juror expresses an unwillingness to seriously consider execution as a punishment, he or she is not permitted to serve on a capital jury. From the much smaller pool of death-qualified jurors, prosecuting and defense attorneys challenge and attempt to exclude jurors whom they perceive as unsympathetic to their case.

In an attempt to counterbalance the perceived one-sidedness of the death qualification process, some states later began to allow for the exclusion of jurors whose strong support for the death penalty would prevent them from voting for a sentence of life in prison. In 1992, in the case of *Morgan v. Illinois*, the Supreme Court ruled that potential jurors who say they would automatically impose the death penalty should also be excluded from capital juries. Although adding on a "life qualification" question superficially appears to balance out the bias created by "death qualification," the number of people unwilling to consider a sentence of LWOP is far smaller (roughly twelve times less) than the number of people unwilling to consider a sentence of death (Miller & Hayward, 2008). One prominent researcher summarized decades of research on capital jury selection in this way:

> With few exceptions, jury selection appears to have succeeded in eliminating jurors unmistakably opposed to capital punishment but fails to eliminate jurors who voice a pro-death penalty stand. (Bowers et al., 2014, p. 436)

In practice, judges have wide latitude in determining just how strong a juror's death penalty reservations must be. For example, a man who said that he would support the ultimate penalty for a criminal who "was in my home, [and] killed my children" but that he would "prefer to see a person rehabilitated" and that he "didn't know if he could push for the death penalty" was disqualified from jury service for not being comfortable enough with a possible death sentence (*Morrison v. State*, 2002).

Jurors naturally try to make sense of the odd process of death qualification. Mere exposure to the process suggests to jurors that the legal system disapproves of people who are opposed to capital punishment and that both the defense and prosecutors anticipate a conviction and a death sentence (Haney, 2005). More generally, the process of death qualification skews the demographic and attitudinal composition of the jury, which in turn shapes how jurors interpret and respond to evidence. Because African Americans and women are significantly more likely to oppose capital punishment, they are significantly more likely to be excluded from capital jury service. African Americans are already underrepresented in most jury pools, and the process of death qualification reduces their numbers even further (Paternoster & Brame, 2008; Swafford, 2011). Democrats, low-income persons, and people who oppose the death penalty on religious grounds are also more likely to be excluded from serving on capital juries (Yelderman et al., 2016).

Attitudes relevant to the criminal justice system are strongly correlated with attitudes about politics and social order. Compared to excluded jurors, jurors who survive the death qualification process are significantly more punishment-oriented, less worried about convicting the innocent, less likely to be concerned that capital punishment might be unfair to minorities, and more likely to judge penalty phase evidence as aggravating rather than mitigating. Ultimately, as compared to non-death qualified jurors, death qualified jurors are more likely to find the defendant guilty and more likely to favor a sentence of death over a sentence of life in prison. Both "conviction-proneness" and "death-proneness" have been demonstrated in several studies (Foglia & Sandys, 2018; Haney et al., 2022). Those jurors who "pass" the death qualification test tend to filter evidence through beliefs and preconceptions that favor the prosecution.

Victim Impact Testimony in the Penalty Phase

The victims of crimes testify in many types of criminal trials, usually to describe the details of the alleged crime. But because capital trials always involve a murder, the victim cannot testify at trial. Instead, during the penalty phase of the trial in which the jury must decide if the defendant should be sentenced to life imprisonment or death, members of the victim's family (who are sometimes referred to as "co-victims") are usually allowed to make statements about the continuing impact of the murder (Mitchell et al., 2015). These *victim impact statements* (VIS) can be made in court, via video, or in written documents. In principle, such statements serve to inform the jury about the extensive and ongoing suffering caused by the defendant's crimes.

The decision to allow VISs in capital trials was a reversal of the long-standing principle that one aim of the legal system was to minimize the emotionality of legal decision-making. Since colonial times, "the 'impassionate' hand of the state was meant to punish offenders without a personal or emotional agenda" (Kaufman, 2020). For decades, the Supreme Court viewed VISs as inherently damaging to the ideal of impartial, rational sentencing decisions. For example, in the case of *Booth v. Maryland* (1987), the Court held that,

> [o]ne can understand the grief and anger of the family caused by the brutal murders in this case, and there is no doubt that jurors are aware of these feelings. But the formal presentation of this information by the state can serve no other purpose than to inflame the jury and divert it from deciding the case on the relevant evidence concerning the crime and the defendant. (*Booth v. Maryland*, 1987, p. 508)

The Court also worried that the introduction of VISs might sway jurors to base their penalty decisions on the perceived value of the victim rather than on the nature of the crime and the characteristics of the defendant. Justice Douglas observed that the court did not want to convey the message that

> defendants whose victims were assets to their community are somehow more deserving of punishment than those whose victims are perceived to be less worthy . . . our system of justice does not tolerate such distinctions. (*Booth v. Maryland*, 1987, p. 506)

But, only a few years later, the Court changed its mind. In *Payne v. Tennessee* (1991), the Court ruled that VISs were admissible in capital sentencing trials. The Court decided it was fair to use VISs to emphasize the victim's "uniqueness as an individual human being." Part of the reasoning was that, although no information about the victim's character or the impact of the victim's death on survivors was presented in capital trials, the defense was permitted to present information about the defendant (e.g., mental impairment or mental illness, or a childhood filled with abuse and neglect) in the form of mitigating circumstances. The *Payne* decision was, in part, intended to rebalance a system that the Court believed "unfairly weighted the scales in a capital trial" in favor of the defendant (Pitt, 2013). Still later, in *Bosse v. Oklahoma* (2016), the Court clarified that VISs should not include statements about the defendant and pleas to impose a sentence of death.

It warrants mention that, although it may be true that most co-victims prefer that the murderer who killed their loved one be sentenced to death, not all survivors argue in favor of death. Here are two examples:

He is an evil creature, who I would condemn to many, many long years of anguish and despair. He doesn't deserve a quick, painless, humane death . . . a humane death penalty should be reserved for killers who are capable of honest remorse. (Szmania & Gracyalny, 2006, p. 238)

He's an animal. I don't wish for him to die, I wish for him to have a long, suffering, cruel death. Hopefully terminal cancer. (Szmania & Gracyalny, 2006, p. 238)

Whether or not it is relevant or fair to allow VISs is a matter of continuing controversy. A central issue is "perceived victim quality." If a victim is portrayed as a valued and virtuous person by his or her survivors, that victim might elicit more sympathy than victims who don't have such advocates or victims whose lives were less virtuous. Moreover, if the person delivering the VIS is especially eloquent in describing the victim and articulating the anguish caused by the murder, their statement is likely to have more impact. This difference in the perceived quality of the victims might result in unequal treatment of defendants convicted of the very same crime. Jurors who hear VISs tend to feel greater anger toward the defendant and more empathy for the victim. These feelings shift the sentencing choice toward death (Butler, 2008; Paternoster & Deise, 2011; Myers et al, 2018).

Of course, testimony by members of the victim's family is highly emotional. Bereaved people often sob on the stand, and it is not uncommon for others in the courtroom—including jurors—to weep when hearing such testimony. Grieving family members may describe the admirable qualities of the victim, their love for the victim, and the devastating, ongoing trauma created by the murder. The profound grief of the victim's family is easy for jurors to understand and empathize with. The concern is that this natural, powerful empathic response will translate into a felt obligation to support the harshest sentencing option. Here is how one researcher described the influence of a VIS in a capital trial she observed:

Not only were audience members and jurors openly emotive when co-victims testified, but courtroom staff and judges visibly supported victims. This went beyond discreet looks of empathy, glasses of water, and pats on the arm, which were plentiful and understandable. In many trials, the court as an institution seemed to grant legitimacy to the victims' position. (Kaufman, 2020, p. 179)

Finally, victim impact testimony has both an immediate impact on jurors when it is presented and perhaps additional impact when it is later highlighted in the closing arguments of prosecutors. Here is an excerpt from one prosecutor's final argument:

> Focus on the unspeakable hell that he [the defendant] put those families through . . . because of that man, because he decided to go hunting on the streets of this city, those people's families have nothing left to hug but memories, and we're asking you to remember them. (Kaufman, 2020, p. 173)

Beginning in the late 1990s, some courts began to allow *execution impact statements* (EISs) during the penalty phase (Wolff & Miller, 2009). Such statements are used to explain the severe negative impact that a death sentence would have on the family of the defendant. EISs serve as a counterweight to the perspective presented in VISs. An EIS may bolster the mitigating evidence presented during the penalty phase by including mention of the defendant's difficult life and personal characteristics (e.g., mental impairment or mental illness). More directly, an EIS might encourage jurors to consider the possibility that a death sentence would increase the suffering of the defendant's family and friends (Beck et al., 2007; Wolff & Miller, 2009).

Just as VISs enable the families of victims to play an expanded role in the justice system, EISs allow the families of the defendant to play an expanded role. Many legal scholars argue that EISs restore some balance to the legal system by countering the highly emotional and often persuasive VISs (Thomas, 2000). Because the US Supreme Court has not yet ruled on the admissibility of EISs in capital sentencing trials, the decision to allow EISs is made on a state-by-state basis (Paternoster & Deise, 2011).

The Role of the Defense and the Prosecution in the Penalty Phase

During the penalty phase the defense presents mitigating testimony. Such testimony is not meant to excuse the defendant's violence—he has already been convicted, and, at minimum, he will spend the rest of his life in prison. The testimony is offered to create understanding, to elicit feelings of compassion, and to offer jurors reasons to vote for life in prison instead of the execution chamber. One defender put it this way in his penalty-phase closing argument:

> The reason I wanted you to know as much as possible about [the defendant] is that all the factors in his life in some way determined what happened. All of us are born in this society with certain potentials, certain capacities, certain possibilities. Some of us are born into a certain family, a certain environment and all of these determine the choices we have as we grow up. (Costanzo & Peterson, 1994)

Depending on the characteristics of the case, several forms of mitigation—such as intellectual impairment, emotional distress, abuse and neglect, mental illness, youth at the time of the crime, drug abuse, domination by others—might be presented by defenders. In addition to hearing about terrible murders described in graphic detail, jurors often hear about the disturbing world of the defendant. Many of the people who end up on trial for capital murder have grown up in an environment seething with violence. Attorneys often locate the roots of violence in harrowing experiences of physical and psychological abuse. Defendants in capital murder trials have often suffered from a harsh and punishing life that includes abuse, neglect, and a lack of options. Here is an excerpt from a different closing argument describing the childhood of one defendant:

> You heard about a father that beat the hell out of his mother . . . choked her unconscious. You heard about an alcoholic father, an alcoholic mother. You've heard about, worst of all, an overbearing, arrogant, abusive, nasty, giant brute of a grandfather. . . . Or how about the grandmother that likes to go beating up people with electric extension cords? Or how about torture? . . . Can you imagine the terror of being closed inside a burlap sack, having a rope tied to the burlap sack, having it thrown over a limb of an oak tree and having yourself hoisted. And then being smoked. . . . Can you imagine the terror of that? Does that give you a little bit of a clue of what his life must have been like? To give you a little bit of a clue why the defendant maybe doesn't see things the way we see things? (Costanzo & Peterson, 1994)

The type of mitigation emphasized by the defender depends on the characteristics of the defendant and the crime. In some cases, the circumstances of the crime suggest mental illness. As a different defender explained,

[the defendant] is mentally disturbed. You know it. I know it. . . . Carrying the body of your dead lover around for a couple of weeks in your apartment, lighting fires and talking to her. Sure, any normal human being does that. He's very, very sick, and he has been for a long, long time. Death is an absolute punishment. And we, at least in this country, don't kill people that are not absolutely responsible. (Costanzo & Peterson, 1994)

Heavy use of alcohol or drugs is sometimes cited as a reason to assign less responsibility to the defendant.

Isn't that what alcohol and drugs do to you? They impair your ability to be a rational person, to think properly, to act right. That's why we're concerned about people who take drugs and drink in excess. And throughout the period of time when [the defendant] is involved in the planning of this, his mind is affected. His judgment is impaired by alcohol and by drugs. (Costanzo & Peterson, 1994)

It is hoped that such context helps to explain the defendant's crimes and helps jurors to look beyond the crimes and see the humanity of the defendant.

Prosecutors paint a very different picture of the defendant and his crimes. If the defender's job is to humanize the defendant, the prosecutor's job is to dehumanize him. Of course, this is a far easier task given the savage nature of the defendant's crimes. In their closing arguments, prosecutors attempt to diminish, dispute, or dismiss the importance of whatever has been offered as mitigation. For example,

He had a bad childhood, the bad childhood stuff, ... Is that unusual? . . . Being molested as a kid is not unusual. Being beaten as a kid or hit by your dad or parents or stepfather isn't unusual, and those people don't 30 years later have the Boston Strangler come sprinting out of them. (Costanzo & Peterson, 1994)

Prosecutors may also suggest to jurors that it might be legitimate to dismiss or minimize the importance of some mitigating factors.

> Take alcoholism: does it mean life in prison? One person might say "yes," he wouldn't have committed the crime if he was in his right mind. Another person might say, I know plenty of people who drink and do not commit capital murder. I think he's going to drink and kill again. Or take mental disability. Again, it is up to you. Some people might say, I know lots of people with a mental disability and they don't commit capital murder. . . . Age can be a mitigating factor. You might say, he's young, he deserves a second chance. Or you might look at it and say, if he's already doing this, there's no telling what he might do in his thirties, forties, and fifties. (Kaufman, 2020, p. 106)

According to many prosecutors, mental disturbance is usually more apparent than real.

> What did the [defendants] live for? . . . For the immediate pleasures of life . . . go home sometime and look up the definition of hedonism. It wasn't because of some mental immaturity or mental problem or psychological difficulty. (Costanzo & Peterson, 1994)

Prosecutors also attempt to discount the importance of mitigation by emphasizing free will.

> He has made choices, that's what put him here, the choices he has made. Don't relieve him of responsibility for the choices he has made. . . . At every choice, at every decision-making place, what has he done? He has chosen violence. As a thinking adult you take responsibility for your actions. And your actions have consequences. (Costanzo & Peterson, 1994)

It is often the crimes themselves—murders so vile that they defy understanding—that provide the most powerful aggravation. Especially vicious features of the crime are recounted in vivid detail by prosecutors. When the penalty phase begins, the defendant has already been convicted of a horrible crime, and jurors want severe and certain punishment. While prosecutors may argue that death is the only fitting punishment and that jurors should "show the defendant exactly the compassion and sympathy and understanding he showed his victim," defenders argue that life in prison is sufficiently harsh punishment.

> You couldn't be lenient in this case if you wanted to be. There's no way. The law will not allow it. Personalize a little bit and think about spending the rest of your life in a six-foot by eight-foot room with a toilet in the middle. A room that's about the size of your family bathroom. Think about that. Living in your bathroom for the rest of your life.

Attorneys also make broad philosophical and religious arguments in their final appeals to the jury. Prosecutors emphasize the legitimacy of revenge.

> [The defendant] has victimized completely innocent people. And those people deserve your attention. They deserve to be avenged. That is a very legitimate concept. I would not tell you that vengeance can be separated from what you're doing here. I would not tell you that there isn't a certain amount of anger, of retribution, that is part of a decision that you make, if you decide with death. (Costanzo & Peterson, 1994)

In contrast, defenders urge jurors to show mercy by linking their appeals to religious values. They implore jurors to be guided by loftier values such as compassion and by religious teachings that counsel mercy and condemn revenge.

> Do to the defendant what God did to Cain when he slew Abel. He banished him. Didn't kill him, he banished him. And, that's what you will do to [the defendant]. You will banish him forever. (Costanzo & Peterson, 1994)

There is a stark contrast between the life stories of defendants told by defenders and prosecutors in the penalty phase. Defenders tell a complex and textured story. The defendant is a tragically flawed character, emotionally and socially deformed by years of neglect and abuse. The origins of his violent behavior can be traced back to early life experiences as well as powerful forces acting on him at the time of the crime (e.g., drug addiction, domination by others, mental deficiencies, emotional upheaval). The causes of his crimes are varied and complex. In the prosecutor's contrasting version of the story, both plot and character are simplified. All that is important to know about the character of the defendant is revealed in his brutal crimes. He is an evil, remorseless monster, motivated by little more than greed, rage, or sadism. His crimes have little to do with any suffering in his past; they are the product of a series of free choices. The brutality of the crime and the suffering of the victims cry out for a sentence of death. Finally, defenders emphasize that the law allows for mercy and that jurors must bear the full weight of personal responsibility for the penalty decision. Prosecutors argue that the law allows for the ultimate punishment and that, given the nature and heinousness of the crime, only a sentence of death is proportionate.

Jurors in Capital Murder Trials

Capital jurors find themselves in an extraordinary situation. They are plucked from their daily routines and asked to listen for weeks or months to lawyers, witnesses, and a judge. They are passive spectators of the courtroom proceedings—ritualistic events that are tightly controlled by an esoteric system of rules that most jurors cannot hope to understand fully. They hear about the grisly details of a horrible crime, they hear the heart-wrenching testimony of those who loved the victim, and they hear about the often barren and brutal life of the defendant. They are not allowed to talk with lawyers or witnesses or even to ask the simplest of questions. They are expected to absorb information without participating in the search. They cannot discuss the impending decision with spouses, friends, or family members until after the decision has been made. They cannot even discuss the case with each other until official deliberations commence. In the somewhat euphemistic language of the Court, the capital jury "is made up of individuals placed in a very unfamiliar situation and called on to make a very difficult and uncomfortable choice" (*Caldwell v. Mississippi*, 1985, p. 333). That is, with the help of eleven other people, each capital juror must struggle to decide whether another human being should be killed.

The extraordinary experience of learning about the gruesome details of horrible crimes, hearing from the families of victims and the defendant, and then making a life-or-death decision appear to have strong and lasting effects on most jurors. For example, a juror described the experience of seeing autopsy photos in this way:

[T]he picture with her dead, her eyes open. That was another shocking thing. . . . They had a slide show, and this one slide showed the victim with her eyes open. You thought for a minute that it was her at some time in her life when she was alive, but then they tell you this is a morgue shot. . . . Here is this lifelike looking face looking at you, but this person is dead. That kinda bothered me. (Antonio, 2008, pp. 402)

Another juror, described her continuing, intrusive thoughts related to the trial:

I'm paranoid, I can't shake it. Twice, I ran into a fellow who looked like him (the defendant). I flipped out. I got hysterical, shook and just ran. . . . I dreamed he broke into my apartment on several occasions. (Pappas, 2015)

Other jurors identified the interpersonal strains of trying to reach a group decision during deliberation as a major source of stress.

I had a part in it. I hate it. I hate that I had a part in it.
I just felt a lot of pressure and I went home crying one night.
You had somebody's life in your hands—it's a very big decision.
You had to argue to make the decision . . . continual arguing, tempers
    flared. You could see that over the days it was taking its toll. (Fleury-
    Steiner, 2007, p. 22)

Although research on this topic is limited, those who have looked at the after-effects of capital jury service have found evidence of negative effects, including nightmares, regret, depression, increased drug use, relationship problems, paranoia, and physical distress (Antonio, 2008; Burgason, 2018). The prevalence and duration of these problems among capital jurors is not yet known.

The instructions given to jurors at the end of the penalty phase are, at the heart of the system, designed to restrain and guide the discretion of jurors. Jurors still have considerable discretion, but far less than they had before the *Gregg* decision. The Supreme Court hung its hopes for fair death sentencing on the instructions that jurors carry with them to deliberation. It was assumed that the "lawless," "arbitrary," and "capricious" sentencing condemned in *Furman* would be repaired by using systematic, logical instructions. The complex and varied testimony presented during the penalty phase would be filtered through the clarifying lens of penalty phase instructions, and a probing moral analysis would be transformed into a methodical fact-finding mission.

The instructions are all that jurors have at their disposal to structure their deliberations. The instructions enumerate the legally relevant factors to be considered by jurors. The law tells jurors, "You shall consider, take into account, and be guided by the following factors, if they are applicable." The list of factors varies a bit from state to state, but the following list is representative:

a. The circumstances of the crime[s] of which the defendant was convicted in this case and any special circumstances that were found to be true.
b. Whether or not the defendant has engaged in violent criminal activity other than the crime[s] of which the defendant was convicted in this case. Violent criminal activity is criminal activity involving the unlawful use, attempt to use, or direct or implied threat to use force or violence against a person. [The other violent criminal activity alleged in this case will be described in these instructions.]
c. Whether or not the defendant has been convicted of any prior felony other than the crime[s] of which (he/she) was convicted in this case.
d. Whether the defendant was under the influence of extreme mental or emotional disturbance when (he/she) committed the crime[s] of which (he/she) was convicted in this case.
e. Whether the victim participated in the defendant's homicidal conduct or consented to the homicidal act.
f. Whether the defendant reasonably believed that circumstances morally justified or extenuated (his/her) conduct in committing the crime[s] of which (he/she) was convicted in this case.
g. Whether at the time of the murder the defendant acted under extreme duress or under the substantial domination of another person.
h. Whether, at the time of the offense, the defendant's capacity to appreciate the criminality of (his/her) conduct or to follow the requirements of the law was impaired as a result of mental disease, defect, or intoxication.
i. The defendant's age at the time of the crime[s] of which (he/she) was convicted in this case.
j. Whether the defendant was an accomplice to the murder and (his/her) participation in the murder was relatively minor.

k. Any other circumstance, whether related to these charges or not, that lessens the gravity of the crime[s] even though the circumstance is not a legal excuse or justification. These circumstances include sympathy or compassion for the defendant or anything you consider to be a mitigating factor, regardless of whether it is one of the factors listed above.

Superficially, these "guided discretion" instructions seemed an elegant solution to the problems raised in *Furman*. But just below the orderly surface of the sentencing instructions lies a deep well of ambiguity. For example, when does one infer an "implied threat to use force or violence"? What constitutes "extreme mental or emotional disturbance"? If a victim was fighting with the defendant before his or her death, does that qualify as "participation in the murder"? How much duress is "extreme" and how much domination is "substantial"? There is also room for interpretation as to whether a particular factor is aggravating or mitigating. For example, if a defendant commits a murder in his early twenties, does his age increase or decrease the gravity of his crime? If the defendant was drunk at the time of the crime or if he was easily dominated by accomplices, does this make him more or less dangerous? And what if most of the factors given in the instructions are simply not applicable to a particular case? What if the defendant was physically abused over the course of his childhood? Is this a significant form of mitigation? And what if his early life was spent in a severely impoverished environment? What if his parents simply did not care for or nurture him during his formative years?

To further complicate the "guidance" given to jurors, instructions include a description of how the aggravating and mitigating factors should be combined. A weighing metaphor is to be used.

The weighing of aggravating and mitigating circumstances does not mean the mere mechanical counting of factors on each side of an imaginary scale, or the arbitrary assignment of weights to any of them. You are free to assign whatever moral or sympathetic value you deem appropriate to each and all of the various factors you are permitted to consider. In weighing the various circumstances, you simply determine under the relevant evidence which penalty is justified and appropriate by considering the totality of the aggravating with the totality of the mitigating circumstances. To return a judgment of death, each of you must be persuaded that the aggravating circumstances are so substantial in comparison with mitigating circumstances that it warrants death instead of life without parole. (California Criminal Jury Instructions [CALCRIM], 2023)

If, after reading the instructions, you have a clear understanding of what factors are to be considered and how those factors should be combined, you are doing better than most jurors. Jurors attempt, often unsuccessfully, to interpret the meaning of key terms and phrases. To achieve some understanding, they often use rough translations.

To twelve people off the street, to use the word "willful" versus "deliberate" versus "intentional"—all that becomes very foggy and gray and just sort of burns off in the sun. . . . Did he do it? Yeah. Did he mean it? Yeah. That's what people on the jury broke it down to. (Costanzo & Costanzo, 1994, p. 160)

Key terms in the sentencing instructions are also poorly understood. Here is how jurors from two different trials put it:

The worst thing was that we weren't clear on those instructions. We had to decide from them, pick them apart to understand what they meant. They weren't clear . . . and we were all very tired and stressed out. (Barner, 2014, p. 6)
The first thing we asked for after the instruction was, could the judge define mitigating and aggravating circumstances. Because the different verdicts that we could come up with depended on if mitigating outweighed aggravating or if aggravating outweighed mitigating, or all of that. So we wanted to make sure. I said, "I don't know that I exactly understand what it means." And then everybody else said, "No, neither do I," or "I can't give you a definition." So we decided we should ask the judge. Well, the judge wrote back and said, "You have to glean it from the instructions." (Haney et al., 1994)

Judges are loath to offer any clarification beyond the vague charge of the jury instructions. When juries request further clarification about what criteria to use or how to combine the factors, most judges give a useless response: "I again will emphasize that there are no further criteria other than the instructions that have previously been given to you, and I will read the instructions to you again." The Supreme Court has approved this evasive response (*Weeks v. Angelone*, 2000). Judges are understandably reluctant to clarify or elaborate on the standard instructions because any alteration could later form the basis of an appeal.

Capital jurors are in dire need of clear guidance. In making the logical inferences necessary to find a defendant guilty of a crime, jurors can rely on logic and evidence. But rules of logic are wholly inadequate to the task of deciding whether a defendant deserves to die. Jurors must assess the ultimate value of the person whose life hangs in the balance. Answering the question of whether a person deserves to die for his crimes leads jurors into deep and murky philosophical waters. The sentence depends on the collective capacity of the jurors to engage in complex moral inquiry. They must decide when killing a defendant is justified and when it is not. The mitigating factors presented during the penalty phase and the receptivity of jurors to those factors is all that stands between a defendant and the execution chamber.

The guided-discretion statutes were intended to restrain the "unbridled discretion" that presumably led to a capricious, arbitrary, and discriminatory pattern of death sentencing. But if the instructions given after the penalty trial are not clear and useful, it is unlikely that death sentencing is now rational and unbiased. Unfortunately, the Court's confidence in the system was founded on their own untested (and often unstated) assumptions about the process of jury decision-making. Although these assumptions may seem superficially reasonable, the only important question is how real jurors in capital cases make use of guidance provided by courts. Unfortunately, research indicates that the pattern of death verdicts remains discriminatory despite the Court's efforts to restrain the discretion of jurors. Jurors cannot be effectively guided if the guidance provided by the Court is ineffective.

The Misconceptions of Supreme Court Justices and Capital Jurors

Much of what we know about capital jurors comes from the pioneering work of the Capital Jury Project (CJP). In a multiyear project, CJP researchers conducted in-depth post-trial interviews with 1,198 capital jurors from 353 separate trials in 14 states (Bowers et al., 2014; Foglia & Sandys, 2018). Their findings revealed that, contrary to the expectations and intentions of the Supreme Court, many capital jurors misunderstand the penalty phase instructions and their appointed role in the penalty decision. Perhaps the most fundamental finding of the CJP is that jurors have serious difficulty understanding and following the penalty phase jury instructions (Bentele & Bowers, 2001). Specifically, many jurors struggle with and misinterpret the meaning of aggravating and mitigating factors. As one juror put it,

> I don't think an attorney even knows what the heck this stuff is . . . and it wasn't explained to us, and this was the most important thing. . . . The way this stuff is worded is because that's how the law books told them they have to word it. But that wasn't told to us . . . and we're sitting here thinking that they [the court] tried to trick us. (Barner, 2014, p. 847)

The meaning of "mitigation" and how much weight should be given to mitigating factors is particularly poorly understood. These misunderstandings lead jurors to discount the importance of mitigating factors and tilt the scale toward a death sentence (Bowers et al., 2010). Furthermore, the abstruseness of the penalty phase instructions tends to amplify racial bias. It appears that poor instruction comprehension allows racial prejudice against African Americans to seep into the decision-making process (Lynch & Haney, 2009; Shaked-Schroer et al., 2008). When provided with only vague guidance on how to make the decision, jurors tend to lean more heavily on preexisting beliefs and biases.

Other findings are similarly distressing. The Supreme Court intended for jurors to suspend any judgment about sentencing until after the conclusion of the penalty phase. However, research by the CJP indicates that many jurors have already formed a strong sentencing preference before the penalty phase even begins. By the conclusion of the guilt phase, about 30% of jurors had already decided on death sentence, and about 19% had already decided that the sentence should be life (Bowers et al., 2014). Jurors also misunderstand the centrality of their role in the sentencing decision. Instead of assuming personal responsibility for the sentencing decision, many jurors reported that the law *required* that they vote for death (Bentele & Bowers, 2001). Only 14.4% believed that individual jurors or the jury collectively bore primary responsibility for the penalty decision (Bowers et al., 2003). Moreover, rather than thinking in terms of personal responsibility, jurors emphasized the importance of reaching consensus and tended to discuss the sentencing decision in terms of the group's interpersonal dynamics. Accordingly, jurors did not necessarily feel that they had chosen the best sentence, but they did feel that they had chosen the only possible sentence given the composition of their jury (Bowers et al., 2014; Costanzo & Costanzo, 1994; Sundby, 2010).

One final insight from research on actual capital trials: Although jurors are asked to choose between LWOP and death, most jurors wrongly believe that unless they vote for a death sentence, the defendant will be eligible for parole and may eventually be released from prison. Here are some quotes from jurors who share this belief:

> Life imprisonment, even though it now says, "without possibility of parole," we were still concerned that someday he'd get out on parole. (Foglia and Sandys, 2018)
>
> If you give him life imprisonment, he's going to get out. We all knew that. We talked about that. . . . It's that simple. The only way I can guarantee that [he will stay in prison] is to vote the death penalty. (Costanzo & Costanzo, 1994, p. 163)
>
> Even if we vote for death, he would probably never be put to death. He was going to be on death row probably 'til he dies. But death was the only way to keep him in prison. (Bowers et al., 2010, p. 1149)

There is a strong, reasonable fear among jurors that convicted murderers will continue to be violent in the future (Bowers et al., 2010). This fear leads many jurors to vote for death because they are afraid that if they vote for LWOP, the murderer may later be released and commit another act of violence. These fears also play a critical role in the dynamics of broader public support for the death penalty (see Chapter 4).

The Appeals Process

Appellate review in capital cases is uniquely elaborate. Trials resulting in a sentence of death are subject to more rigorous scrutiny by higher courts because the consequence of an error—executing an innocent person—is grave and irrevocable. If a person serving a life sentence is found to have been wrongfully convicted, he can be released from prison. But if an innocent person is killed by the state, that person cannot be resurrected.

Death sentences are automatically appealed, either to an intermediate appeals court or to the state court of last resort, which is usually called the *state supreme court*. These courts evaluate whether there were legal or procedural errors at trial that might have changed the outcome of the case. If a state supreme court identifies harmful errors at trial, it can order a new trial. But that outcome is exceedingly rare. Once a defendant has been found guilty of capital murder and a jury has sentenced that defendant to death, appellate courts seem to treat those decisions with "a degree of reverence or sacredness that should rarely be cast aside" (Griffin & Griffin, 2018, p. 400). As with many aspects of the death penalty, there are variations among states. For example, Indiana and Kentucky allow capital defendants to waive their rights to appeal, and some states (South Dakota and Tennessee) require an automatic appeal only for sentencing, but not for errors at trial. Even if both the conviction and the sentence are affirmed by a state supreme court, more traditional appeals may be possible in state courts. Usually, such appeals must focus on legal claims or procedural errors not considered during the automatic appeal.

After state appellate court appeals have been exhausted, a person sentenced to death has the right to file a *habeas corpus* (Latin for "you have the body") petition to a federal appeals court. Federal *habeas* petitions must be confined to alleged violations of constitutional rights, such as the right to due process (Fourteenth Amendment), the prohibition against cruel and unusual punishment (Eighth Amendment), and the right to effective assistance of counsel (Sixth Amendment). These appeals can raise issues that go beyond the trial record, including newly discovered evidence, fairness of the trial, jury bias, tainted evidence, incompetence of defense counsel, and prosecutorial misconduct. Finally, a request to be heard can be filed with the US Supreme Court. The US Supreme Court very rarely grants such requests because a broad constitutional issue must be at stake.

When a sentence has been upheld by the state supreme court, an execution warrant may be issued. The date of execution is generally set for not less than sixty days after the warrant has been issued. If appeals are pending, the defendant must apply for a stay of execution. The power to stay executions and commute death sentences rests with the courts, the state governor, or a board of pardons.

It is important to note that political considerations enter the appeals process at several points. Many key decision-makers—district attorneys, judges (including state supreme court justices in some states), and state governors—are elected and usually hope to be reelected. In a pro death penalty state, if a district attorney decides not to seek the death penalty in a high-profile murder case, a judge overturns a death sentence, or a governor commutes a death sentence, their political careers might be hobbled.

Political opponents will use such decisions to portray the prosecutor, judge, or governor as "soft on crime." That dreaded label could make the difference between victory and defeat in the next election.

After the trial, after the appeals have been exhausted, and after long years of confinement on death row, the execution date finally arrives. The nature of life on death row, the effects of living on death row, and the rituals and procedures used to kill condemned prisoners are the subjects of Chapter 5.

3

Does the Death Penalty Deter Potential Murderers?

THE THEORY IS SIMPLE AND intuitively appealing: Fear of the execution chamber will restrain potential murderers. Knowing that they could face the executioner, those who would otherwise kill will stop short of killing. Innocent lives will be saved.

The theory is called *deterrence*. It has served as a compelling justification for the death penalty since ancient times. Deterrence is seemingly self-evident because it is an elaboration of what we know to be true in our own lives: If the potential punishment for a particular behavior is great, we are likely to avoid that behavior. For example, if you work downtown where parking spaces are scarce, you may occasionally risk a $50 fine for parking illegally. But if the fine is raised to $1,000, only the wealthy will be undeterred. Common sense tells us that the death penalty deters. But common sense also tells us that the Earth holds still and the Sun moves across the sky. Only after looking at the evidence do we become convinced that we live on a spinning planet that slowly circles the sun.

As capital punishment became morally troubling to many Americans, the justification of deterrence gained prominence. It offered a seemingly scientific rationale for executions. Supporters of capital punishment were not out for primitive revenge: they were simply discouraging future murders and thereby protecting the public. Moral arguments and quotes from scripture could be bolstered by appeals to reason. Even today, for those who favor dispassionate cost-benefit analyses, deterrence provides a coolly logical basis for favoring executions.

For more than 180 years, researchers have been investigating whether the death penalty serves as a deterrent. The theory of deterrence implies a couple of hypotheses that can be tested by looking closely at murder rates. The first hypothesis is that locations with capital punishment should have lower murder rates than places where execution is not an available sanction. If, for example, one state has the death penalty and a similar, neighboring state does not, the death-penalty state should have proportionately fewer killings. This hypothesis has been thoroughly tested.

The Research Evidence

One of the earliest studies was conducted by a Massachusetts legislator named Robert Rantoul. In the 1840s, Rantoul compiled statistics on murder and execution rates in several nations over a forty-year period. In 1846, he presented his findings: The deterrent effect was illusory. Indeed, his data revealed a counter-deterrence effect.

> Murders have rapidly diminished in those countries in which executions are scarcely known; slightly in France where the change of policy was not so great; while in England, . . . under a milder administration of the law, there has been a change for the better. (Hamilton, 1854, p. 504)

Since Rantoul's time, several hundred studies have been conducted to assess the deterrent power of capital punishment. Nearly all of them lend credence to Rantoul's early conclusions.

Critics of this early research countered that the United States is different from other countries. What failed to work in Europe may be effective here. Indeed, the United States is a useful laboratory for putting deterrence theory to the test. Some states have the death penalty, other states do not. Some states have adopted the death penalty only to abandon it later. Some states have even adopted the death penalty and abolished it later, only to reinstate it even later. Differences between similar states and changes in the same state over time enable researchers to conduct multiple tests of the theory. Specifically, the theory predicts that states with capital punishment will have lower murder rates than states without capital punishment. Of course, it's a bit more complicated because the states being compared must be as similar as possible. Comparing Oregon, Florida, and Delaware might not be especially informative because these three states differ on several important dimensions. A better test—the test used in the research literature—uses geographically adjacent states that tend to share many features including history, culture, and economy. In the 1960s, a sociologist named Thorsten Sellin made just such comparisons. Supporters of capital punishment found no comfort in his findings.

Sellin examined clusters of states that were similar in most respects. He found, for example, that North Dakota, a state without the death penalty, had a lower homicide rate than two similar states that did have the death penalty, South Dakota and Nebraska. Michigan, a non-capital punishment state, had a nearly identical murder rate to Indiana, and a lower rate than Ohio, both of which had the death penalty. Rhode Island, a state that only had the penalty of life imprisonment, was compared to two death-penalty states, Massachusetts and Connecticut. Rhode Island's murder rate was lower than Connecticut's and identical to Massachusetts's. To be sure, a couple of states without the death penalty (e.g., Maine) had higher rates than comparable states with the death penalty (e.g., New Hampshire). But overall, the states with execution chambers had rates of murder that were significantly higher than states that did not execute murderers (Sellin, 1980).

But maybe things have changed. After all, Sellin's data examined the years 1920 to 1955. It is possible that changes in American culture or the legal system—especially modifications in the trial process since the *Furman v. Georgia* and *Gregg v. Georgia* decisions—have made the deterrent effect more powerful. Several researchers set out to see if deterrence had changed with the times. Ruth Peterson and William Bailey examined homicide rates for a twelve-year period. Comparing similar, adjacent states, they found that the annual murder rate in states with the death penalty was higher than in states that had abolished it. Specifically, the average murder rate in states with the death penalty was 8.64 for every 100,000 people. In states without the death penalty, the rate was 5.35 (Petersen & Bailey, 1988).

Deterrence theory makes other predictions. A second testable hypothesis has to do with the effects, over time, of getting rid of or bringing back the death penalty. If the death penalty is abandoned in a particular state, murder rates should climb because the fear of execution has been removed. Conversely, if a particular place establishes the death penalty or restores it after a long period of absence, then murder rates should fall. The studies described above included this kind of longitudinal analysis of homicide rates when the death penalty was in effect and when it was suspended for a period of years. These analyses revealed no deterrence effect.

In 1983, Richard Lempert looked for a relationship between the number of executions and number of homicides. He included several states over a fifteen-year period. No relationship was found. His conclusion echoed that of earlier researchers: "The death penalty in general and executions in particular do not deter homicide" (Lempert, 1983, p. 112). A more recent multistate comparison yielded a similar finding—for the twenty-seven states where the death penalty was in effect, six showed a decrease in murder rates, thirteen showed an increase in murder rates, and eight saw no change in murder rates (Shepherd, 2005). The conclusions of studies conducted in the United States have been confirmed by research conducted abroad. Researchers measured the murder rate in twelve countries and two foreign cities before and after abolition of the death penalty. Eight of the fourteen cases (57%) showed a decreased murder rate in the year following abolition, while only five (36%) showed an increase. Furthermore, when they examined longer periods of time, there was even less support for the deterrence hypothesis (Archer & Gartner, 1984). When looking at this research, it is essential to keep in mind that there are two fundamental public-policy questions: Will abolishing the death penalty increase the murder rate? And, will reinstating the death penalty cause the murder rate to drop? Based on the research, the answer to both questions is clearly "no."

But maybe comparisons between death-penalty states and non–death penalty states are inconclusive. Maybe the paired states were different in a variety of unnoticed and unmeasured ways. Maybe even adjacent states aren't similar enough and researchers were comparing apples and oregano. This basic criticism spawned a new wave of deterrence research. This new wave looked at the effect of the death penalty over long periods of time and used complex statistical procedures to control for or remove the impact of factors that might influence the number of murders. By taking into account several factors that were known to contribute to murder rates, researchers hoped to purify and clarify their comparisons.

One of the first studies to make use of such sophisticated statistical controls was conducted by Baldus and Cole in 1975. Like earlier researchers, they looked at contiguous states. But, unlike earlier researchers, they took into account several characteristics known to influence murder rates: unemployment, probability of arrest and conviction, percent of the population between the ages of fifteen and twenty-five, per capita financial expenditures on the police force, and other factors. Even after controlling for such factors, no deterrent effect was found. After scores of studies and decades of data analysis, few people found any reason to believe in deterrence. Things looked bleak for deterrence theorists. Then, in 1975, an economist named Isaac Ehrlich came to their rescue.

Ehrlich argued that most of the previous research failed to consider important differences between states. Using a sophisticated statistical technique called *multiple regression*, he looked at the impact of the death penalty on murder in the United States from 1933 to 1969. Taking into account arrest and conviction rate, unemployment rate, per capita income, population between the ages of fourteen and twenty-four, and other variables, Ehrlich examined what he called "execution risk." This risk was defined as the ratio of executions to convictions for murder. After churning through the data, Ehrlich declared that he had uncovered a powerful deterrent effect (Ehrlich, 1975).

Ehrlich's findings found an enthusiastic audience. Politicians and policymakers who supported the death penalty were eager to embrace any research that reinforced their position. And, at the time, Ehrlich's was the only apparently credible study that had managed to detect any deterrent effect. Even better, Ehrlich's findings could be expressed as a pithy slogan: "Every execution prevents seven or eight murders." This lone pro-deterrence study was also cited in the *Gregg* decision of 1976. Balancing the Ehrlich study against scores of studies that found no deterrent effect, the Supreme Court concluded that

> [s]tatistical attempts to evaluate the worth of the death penalty as a deterrent to crimes by potential offenders have occasioned a great deal of debate. The results simply have been inconclusive. (*Gregg v. Georgia*, 1976, p. 85)

Because of Ehrlich's highly mathematical approach, only other social scientists could discern the flaws in his research. Almost immediately, critiques began to appear in the research literature. A closer look at the data revealed a striking anomaly: When the last few years (1963–1969) were removed from the analysis, the impact of "execution risk" was to increase rather than decrease the number of murders. Other critics pointed out that Ehrlich had failed to include several critical factors in his analysis: rural-to-urban migration, gun ownership, level of violent crime, and length of prison sentences. When these and other key factors were taken into account, the deterrent effect evaporated. The fatal blow to Ehrlich's research came from the prestigious National Academy of Sciences. Their panel (headed by a Nobel Prize–winning economist) reanalyzed Ehrlich's data and concluded that the data showed no deterrent effect (Klein et al., 1978).

As the evidence against deterrence continued to accumulate, some people suggested yet another explanation for the absence of a deterrence effect: Researchers were looking at the wrong factors. What mattered was not whether the death penalty was an available sanction, but the number of executions that were actually carried out. Maybe it takes an actual execution to instill fear in the hearts of potential murderers, and it is only this fear that causes them to refrain from killing. And because it is only actual executions that demonstrate the grave consequences of murder, greater publicity should boost the deterrent effect. According to this line of reasoning, sufficient fear will be felt only when an execution is vivid in people's minds—in the days, weeks, and months immediately following an execution. As the memory of each execution fades in the minds of would-be murderers, the deterrent effect might fade and then finally disappear.

This idea that it is only the actual occurrence of an execution (rather than laws authorizing the death penalty) that deters is by no means new. Back in 1935, Robert Dann tabulated the number of murders sixty days before and sixty days after executions. Interestingly, Dann found that the number of murders *rose* after each execution (Dann, 1935). Supporters of deterrence retreated a bit farther and suggested that maybe only well-publicized executions generated the effect. But scores of studies failed to support even this more limited prediction. For example, David King (1979) looked at twenty well-publicized executions over more than a decade. His findings also ran contrary to the predictions of deterrence theory: On average, each execution produced an increase of 1.2 homicides (King, 1979). In 1990, William Bailey conducted an especially detailed analysis of the impact of television publicity on murder rates. No effect could be detected. Even when type of publicity (e.g., graphic vs. matter-of-fact coverage) was considered, there was no discernable impact on murder rates (Bailey, 1990).

Another issue raised by the defenders of deterrence theory concerned the type of murder for which the death penalty was an available punishment. Many studies of deterrence, especially the older studies, had examined total homicide rates. But not all murders are punishable by death. If we make the dubious assumption that murderers know which types of murders are punishable by death, it is possible that only capital murderers are being deterred. Perhaps the deterrent effect is being masked because non-capital murders are included in the analysis. In response to this criticism, researchers looked at the murder of police officers. This is a useful measure because killing a police officer is punishable by death in every state that permits capital punishment. Moreover, it has often been argued that the death penalty is especially useful for deterring fleeing criminals who are in danger of being arrested. An outspoken supporter of capital punishment, put it this way:

> Without the death penalty, an offender having committed a crime that leads to imprisonment for life has nothing to lose if he murders the arresting officer. By murdering the officer . . . such criminals increase their chances of escape, without increasing the severity of the punishment they will suffer if caught. (Van den Haag & Conrad, 1983, p. 234)

Despite the superficial logic of that argument, there is no evidence that police officers are safer in jurisdictions that have capital punishment (Bailey & Petersen, 1987). In one of the most thorough and sophisticated investigations of the topic, researchers looked at police killings over a fourteen-year period. They analyzed several types of police killings (e.g., on-duty vs. off-duty) and took into account several key variables: the total number of executions, the number of executions for police killings, the amount of media coverage of such executions, and the type of media attention given to these executions. They even removed the influence of variables known to be linked to murder rates (e.g., number of people living in cities, number of persons aged sixteen to thirty-four, divorce rate, unemployment, and percentage of the population on welfare) and employed a variety of statistical techniques. They were still unable to locate a deterrent effect (Bailey & Petersen, 1994).

Brutalization: Does the Death Penalty Incite Murder?

Deterrence theorists have always naively assumed that the threat of the death penalty would suppress the murder rate. The evidence indicates they are wrong. Of course, logic suggests three other possibilities: (1) the death penalty has no effect on murder rates, (2) the death penalty increases the number of murders, and (3) the death penalty deters some types of murder and stimulates other types. It is the second possibility, known as *brutalization*, that we now turn to.

From the beginning, public officials saw signs that the death penalty did not deter. During public executions in early America and Europe, pickpockets feverishly worked the crowds, even though picking pockets was a crime punishable by death.

> The thieves selected the moment when the strangled man was swinging above them as the happiest opportunity, because they knew that everybody's eyes were on that person and all were looking up. (Koestler, 1957, p. 57)

These thieves somehow failed to absorb the intended message of the execution.

Not only did the bloody public executions of the past fail to deter, they also churned up great violence in their wake. That was the principal reason why, despite great popularity, executions were removed from public view. Public executions were the scenes of drunkenness, revelry, fighting, and rioting. From the beginning, the spectacle of killing brought out the worst in people and brought out the worst people. After standing among the spectators at a public execution in 1849, Charles Dickens described the scene:

> I believe that a sight so inconceivably awful as the wickedness and levity of the immense crowd collected at that execution this morning could be imagined by no man. . . . The horrors of the gibbet and of the crime which brought the wretched murderers to it faded in my mind before the atrocious bearing, looks, and language of the assembled spectators . . . thieves, low prostitutes, ruffians, and vagabonds of every kind, flocked on to the ground, with every variety of offensive and foul behaviour . . . thousands of upturned faces, so inexpressibly odious in their brutal mirth or callousness, that a man had cause to feel ashamed of the shape he wore, and to shrink from himself, as fashioned in the image of the Devil. (quoted in Laurence, 1931, p. 190)

The wardens of modern American prisons have long recognized the incendiary potential of executions. Disciplinary problems and violent incidents rise during the days leading up to and following an execution. And the disruptive effects sometimes reach beyond the prison walls. Especially when an infamous killer is executed, rowdy crowds gather near the prison to cheer in approval when the death is announced. It is for these reasons that modern executions are held without fanfare, outside of public view. Unseen executions create fewer disturbances. Although many public officials *say* they believe that executions deter, they *act* as if they believe that executions brutalize.

Like hypotheses about deterrence, hypotheses about brutalization can be tested. A careful examination of the data collected to evaluate deterrence theory should reveal whether brutalization occurs. If there is validity to the claim that executions brutalize, murder rates ought to rise after executions. In a series of articles and books on precisely this question, the respected death-penalty scholar William Bowers has examined data from nearly seventy different studies of murder rates. His conclusion is that executions do increase murder rates and that "this effect is slight in magnitude (though not in consequence), that it occurs within the first month or two of an execution, and that it dissipates thereafter" (Bowers, 1988, p. 71). This small but consequential impact amounts to an average increase of one to four extra murders in the weeks after an execution. Bowers uncovered another intriguing trend: Although the number of murders tends to rise after any execution, the rise is greater when the execution is well publicized. Many other researchers have detected this brutalization effect. For example, a study of the relationship between executions and murders over a sixty-six-year period found that executions lead to an increase of 1 to 1.7 murders on average (Donohue & Wolfers, 2006; 2010).

It could be that executions do communicate an important message. It just isn't the message lawmakers intend to communicate. Apparently, the salient lesson is not "If you take a life, you will lose your life" but instead, "It is acceptable to take the life of someone who has committed an egregious wrong against you." In fact, Bowers argued that the process of identification is likely to work in exactly the opposite direction from the one proposed by deterrence theory.

> The potential murderer may equate someone who has greatly offended him someone he hates, fears, or both—with the executed criminal. . . . Indeed, he himself may identify with the state as avenger; the execution

may justify and reinforce his resolve to exact lethal vengeance. (Bowers, 1988, p. 54)

The psychology of brutalization is not yet entirely understood, but there are clues in the research on aggression and imitation. Perhaps some people with a loose grip on sanity are the ones most influenced by an execution. Media accounts of the execution and stories about the condemned man may bring violent images and ideas to the minds of a few susceptible and potentially violent people. Some of these people may become morbidly obsessed with killing. For those people who are already primed and ready to act violently, fascination with a murder or an execution may be enough to push barely repressed impulses to the surface. Some sociologists and psychiatrists have suggested that persons haunted by self-loathing may even see execution as a means of escape rather than as a dreaded punishment. For such people, the benefits of murder may become salient.

> With the crime that leads to execution, the offender also strikes back at society or particular individuals. The execution will, of course, satisfy a guilt-inspired desire for punishment, and may also be seen as providing the opportunity to be seen and heard, an occasion to express resentment, alienation, and defiance. (Bowers, 1988, p. 56)

The psychological dynamics underlying a brutalization effect need further exploration, but the finding of brutalization is more consistent with the broader research on violence than is a deterrent effect. Certainly, we know that other forms of violence tend to beget more violence: The assassination of John F. Kennedy boosted the homicide rate, and highly publicized suicides (like that of Robin Williams) provoke a measurable increase in suicides (Berkowitz & Macaulay, 1971; Fink et al., 2018; Huesmann, 2018). And, like the brutalization effect of executions, the effects of assassinations and suicides subside after a month or two. The impact of all forms of violence is magnified when the violence receives greater publicity. Politicians supporting the death penalty often declare that the death penalty is worth having even if it only saves a single innocent life. Is the reverse also true? Should the death penalty be abolished if it incites the taking of a single innocent life?

The Final Wave of Deterrence Research?

Research on the possible deterrent and brutalization effects of capital punishment slowed to a relative trickle during the past two decades. Several more large-scale statistical studies were conducted between 1995 and 2015, and a substantial majority of these studies failed to produce findings supporting the deterrence effect. As one review paper put it, the data for the "vast majority of years and the vast majority of states do not support deterrence" (Vito & Vito, 2018, p. 177). One study analyzed data from 1977 to 2006 and found that executions failed to suppress homicides (Kovandzic et al., 2009), while another found a small deterrent effect, but only for homicides that were not eligible for the death penalty (Fagan et al., 2006). Reviews of multiple studies found that neither deterrence nor brutalization effects were large enough to be considered statistically significant (Yang & Lester, 2008) and that executions both increased and decreased murders depending on the conditions imposed by researchers and the statistical methods used to analyze findings (Manski & Pepper, 2013). The source of these somewhat confusing conclusions seems to be the complex statistical approach used by researchers. This approach created several problems in the interpretation of the data. For example, the statistical models created by researchers were highly sensitive to assumptions embedded in those models. Different assumptions yielded divergent conclusions. Estimates of the strength of deterrence or brutalization over time depended on which variables (e.g., number of prison admissions in a region during a specified period of time, the unemployment rate, expenditures on the state judiciary) were included in the model and how heavily each relevant variable was weighted.

In 2012, the highly respected National Research Council (NRC) assembled a team of prominent scholars to evaluate the effect of the death penalty on murder rates. The scholars carefully reviewed all the relevant research and published an analysis of their findings. Their message to researchers offered no comfort to advocates of deterrence or brutalization.

> [C]laims that research demonstrates that capital punishment decreases or increases the homicide rate by a specified amount or has no effect on the homicide rate should not influence policy judgments about capital punishment. (National Research Council [NRC], 2012, p. 2)

The two basic research deficiencies identified by the NRC were (1) that the existing studies were unable to specify if executions produced a brutalization or deterrence effect *beyond* the effect of the alternative punishment of life imprisonment without parole, and (2) the available research relied on the "use of incomplete or implausible models of potential murderers' perceptions of and response to capital punishment" (p. 3). Put differently, a variety of inescapable problems with data quality and data analysis—the relatively small number of executions per year, the sheer number of variables that potentially influence both execution and homicide rates over time, and the assumptions embedded in statistical models that attempt to estimate deterrence effects—render the findings of most studies inconclusive. The NRC also found that—aside from the formidable methodological problems—an equally consequential problem concerned the conceptually thin and highly implausible theory of *how* the death penalty might deter potential murderers. We now turn to the problems with the theory.

The Flawed Theory Underlying a Belief in Deterrence

Perhaps the findings summarized above are unsurprising. After all, the proposition that the death penalty intimidates would-be murderers is based on an implausibly rational model of human behavior. It assumes that potential killers engage in a dispassionate weighing of the costs and benefits of killing. This assumption is simply wrong. Most murders are crimes of passion—committed under the blinding influence of rage, hatred, jealousy, or fear. To be sure, there are some exceptions, the "hit man" or the terrorist or the calculating husband or wife who kills to collect insurance money. But planned, intentional murders are rare, constituting less than 10% of the total (Bowers et al., 1984).

Who, then, is likely to be deterred by the distant threat of the execution chamber? Probably not the person who acts in the heat of passion or the person whose attempt at robbery goes tragically wrong. Certainly not the insane or mentally disturbed killer or the person whose mind is clouded by alcohol or drugs at the time of the murder. Not the young gang member whose whole subculture exalts macho displays and risk-taking. Not the person who kills spontaneously or accidentally in the midst of an altercation; not the murderer who wishes to be caught; not the criminal who believes he can escape arrest or conviction; not the terrorist who seeks fame and martyrdom; not even the cold, calculating murderer who notices that the probability of execution is exceedingly low. A researcher who has studied the residents on death row reminds us that,

> the reality, with few exceptions, is that murderers are not clear-thinking people. They are impulsive, self-centered, often warped; overwhelmingly they are products of violent homes; frequently they are addled by booze or drugs; and most of them are deeply anti-social. The values and sanctions of society don't concern them. They kill out of mental illness, or sexual perversion, for instant gratification or sheer bloody-mindedness. Some murderers actually seem drawn to the death house. (Von Drehle, 1995, p. 209)

Deterrence theory owes its intuitive appeal to the fact that when most of us sit back in cool, rational reflection, we reason that the prospect of facing the executioner might prevent us from acting on the urge to kill. But very few people are engaged in rational reflection when they use a knife, a club, or a gun. Besides, most of us do not belong to the tiny minority of people who will commit a murder. Most of us would not murder even if murder only carried a small punishment. We are not the ones who need to be restrained. Not only do we have a well-developed moral sense, but we have learned to control our baser impulses. We also consider our lives to be worth living, and we have people we care about. We have a lot to lose.

The theory of deterrence rests on other flimsy assumptions. It assumes that capital punishment is *uniquely* deterring, that execution is perceived to be a significantly harsher punishment than life imprisonment without parole. For those few murderers who carefully weigh one possibility against the other, we cannot predict which punishment will be judged to be more frightening. The prospect of being confined in a cage until you die of old age, surrounded by other dangerous criminals, and stripped of the ability to make important choices about how to spend your time, is probably at least as terrifying as the thought of being executed sometime in the distant future. As Cesare Beccaria argued, the "prolonged wretchedness" of a life in prison has a greater impact on the human mind than "the idea of death, which men always see in the hazy distance" (Beccaria, 1764/1963, p. 49).

Some people continue to have faith in the deterrent power of executions despite all evidence to the contrary. They argue that we simply need to do the job better. That is, we should transform the death penalty into an effective deterrent by increasing its severity, certainty, and celerity. Of course, not much can be done to increase severity. We could turn back the clock and revive the torturous practices of breaking at the wheel, burning at the stake, and boiling in oil. But few Americans would countenance such cruelty. And, in fact, there is no evidence that such practices were any more effective as deterrents. We are left with the two options of increasing certainty and celerity.

The penalty of death has never been certain. The US execution rate peaked in 1938, when just over 2% of homicides resulted in executions. We haven't approached that level of certainty since. A return to that historically high level or even a level ten times higher is not likely to cause potential murderers to believe that the risk of execution is high.

We could, however, compress the length of time between conviction and execution. On average, condemned prisoners wait more than eighteen years for their appointment with the executioner (Diaz, 2022). There is no doubt that, in theory, executions could be swifter. But theory always differs from practice. The cost of speedier executions would be high, and the hypothesized increase in deterrence would likely not materialize. Our system of capital punishment has evolved over many decades and should not be dismantled in the vain hope that a few potential murders *might* be deterred. Questionable attempts to create a deterrent effect would also need to be balanced against our tolerance for wrongful conviction and wrongful execution.

The changes in the legal system necessary to boost the deterrent power of capital punishment—simplifying capital trials, dramatically reducing the number of post-conviction appeals, increasing the pain caused by executions, increasing the number of crimes eligible for the death penalty— would be draconian, morally unacceptable, and probably unconstitutional. These reforms would also increase the risk of wrongful conviction and execution while failing to reduce the most common capital crime: spontaneous murder committed in the heat of passion.

With respect to the death penalty, deterrence theory points in one direction and the facts point in the opposite direction. The fragile logic of deterrence theory has crumbled under the weight of research evidence. More than a century of experience and hundreds of research studies lead to an inescapable conclusion: The death penalty does not deter potential murderers. Confronted with the accumulated evidence, people who once made bold claims about the deterrent power of executions have been forced into a long, slow retreat. As each of their arguments was demolished by the facts, deterrence theorists have found new justifications for supporting capital punishment. One keen observer put it this way:

> Proponents [of deterrence] increasingly find themselves affirming more idiosyncratic explanations for the effects they presume the death penalty has, but which research has yet to reveal. . . . With each new set of findings their task becomes more arduous and their arguments become less plausible. (Bowers, 1974, p. 163)

The burden of proof falls squarely on the shoulders of those who still claim to have faith in the power of deterrence. The conclusion that the death penalty does not deter rests on a mountain of evidence built up over many decades. Anyone who manages to detect a deterrent effect must weigh his or her findings against that mountain.

Research on the lack of deterrence will continue to accumulate. And, occasionally, because of a methodological flaw, a statistical anomaly, or an unusual confluence of events during the measured time span, a researcher will trap the elusive deterrent effect. Later, when other researchers look at the same data, the effect will vanish. The supposed deterrent effect of the death penalty now looks more and more like some mythical creature whose existence seems less and less probable. There are still people who long to believe in the myth, and, for them, no amount of data will dislodge their conviction.

Even if there is a miniscule deterrent effect (perhaps for the tiny percentage of murders that are calm and calculated), it is overshadowed by lack of a deterrent effect for most murderers and the potentially destructive effects of brutalization. If a few innocent lives are saved, many more innocent lives may be sacrificed. And if executions lead to the taking of innocent lives, surely the practice of killing murderers should be judged immoral, especially for those whose support of the death penalty rested on the belief that it saves lives.

All but the most irrational supporters of capital punishment have lost faith in deterrence. Many who still believe in deterrence theory will usually abandon their belief when they become aware of the impressive evidence refuting it. But there has always been another group whose professed faith in deterrence was disingenuous. For this group, deterrence is merely a socially acceptable, sanitized reason for supporting the death penalty. Deterrence theory allows them to cloak themselves in rationality and conceal the underlying reasons for their support. Research has now stripped away that cloak and exposed the real reasons for their support of the death penalty: rage and revenge.

4

Does the American Public Support the
Death Penalty?

Articles and News Reports on capital punishment still declare that the penalty of death still enjoys the support of the American public. And, in a limited sense, these reports are true: When asked a general question such as "Are you in favor of the death penalty for persons convicted of murder?" about 54% of Americans declare their support (Gallup, 2022). Apparently, those who believe that capital punishment should be abolished have lost the battle for the hearts and minds of the American public.

This belief in solid public support has consequences. Those who are entrusted to make decisions about the value of the death penalty still justify their decisions by proclaiming that they are carrying out the will of the people. Public opinion on the death penalty not only affects the actions of political candidates and office holders: It also affects the Supreme Court's judgments concerning what does and does not constitute cruel and unusual punishment. Thus, it is vital to understand the dynamics of public opinion on capital punishment.

In 1972, when the US Supreme Court ruled that our system of deciding who should live and who should die was unconstitutionally arbitrary and discriminatory, the Justices looked to community standards for guidance. As Justice Powell explained,

[m]embers of this Court have recognized the dynamic nature of the prohibition against cruel and unusual punishments. The final meaning was

not set in 1791. Rather, . . . the words of the Amendment are not precise, and their scope is not static. The Amendment must draw its meaning from the evolving standards of decency that mark the progress of a maturing society. (*Furman v. Georgia*, 1972, p. 429)

Some Justices relied on public opinion surveys to assess prevailing standards of decency. Other Justices looked to another source of information about community standards: the frequency with which juries handed out sentences of death. This data caused some Justices to conclude that the death penalty violated the moral standards of the time. As Justice Brennan noted,

[t]he objective indicator of society's view of an unusually severe punishment is what society does with it, and today society will inflict death upon only a small sample of the eligible criminals. [Juries] . . . have been able to bring themselves to vote for death in a mere 100 or so cases among the thousands tried each year where the punishment is available. . . . At the very least, I must conclude that contemporary society views this punishment with substantial doubt. (*Furman v. Georgia*, 1972, p. 299)

While the Supreme Court continues to pay some attention to public attitudes, its analyses of these attitudes tend to be cursory and disinterested in underlying dynamics. Justices have often used the very same data to argue contradictory positions. At least for now, most of the Justices have decided that capital punishment does not violate community standards.

But perhaps the Justices, the politicians, the pundits, and the media have misread or misrepresented the public opinion surveys. Even when support for capital punishment appeared strong, it was often characterized as "a mile wide and an inch deep." But levels of support continue to change, and only a more thorough analysis of the data can reveal whether support for the death penalty is fragile or solid, shallow or deep, ephemeral or enduring.

What the Surveys Tell Us

The Gallup Organization began surveying public opinion on the death penalty in December 1936, after unprecedented levels of public attention were directed toward the execution of Bruno Hauptmann, the alleged murderer of the Lindbergh baby. At that time, 61% of those questioned indicated support for the death penalty and 39% indicated opposition (a "no opinion" category was not included). In recent times, the standard question asked is, "Are you in favor of the death penalty for a person convicted of murder?" The pattern of responses to this question has oscillated wildly over the ensuing ninety years. The percentage of Americans favoring capital punishment declined through the 1950s and early 1960s. Support fell to its nadir in 1966, when only 42% favored the death penalty, and it peaked in 1994, when 80% of Americans expressed support. For the past five years the overall level of support has hovered near 55% (Gallup, 2022).

Some demographic characteristics are systematically related to attitudes toward capital punishment. Differences have been found for the categories of race, income, gender, and political orientation. On average, over the past fifty years, White respondents favor the death penalty by a margin of about 27% over Black respondents, and about 3% more Black respondents than White respondents express "no opinion." This is the most enduring demographic divide on attitudes toward capital punishment (Porter et al., 2018). Researchers have attributed this racial divide to the belief among African Americans that the legal system has historically protected the interests of White Americans at the expense of their interests (Baumgartner et al., 2023). Indeed, Black Americans are incarcerated at significantly higher rates than White Americans, and they are disproportionately sentenced to death (see Chapter 7). A generalized distrust of the legal system is also reflected in a greater belief among African Americans that innocent people have been convicted and executed (Butler et al., 2018).

Money also matters. When respondents are partitioned into three income categories—top, middle, and bottom—those in the top income category are 13% more likely than people in the bottom category to support the death penalty. More males than females support the death penalty (by about 9 percentage points), and females are more likely to indicate opposition by a margin of 4%. More college graduates oppose the death penalty than do people with a high school education or less (by about 7 percentage points). Unsurprisingly, political orientation also makes a difference. Republicans favor the death penalty (76%) while Democrats do not (34%). Support is also stronger among people older than fifty-five years and among people living in the South. In sum, the people most likely to support the death penalty are middle- to upper-class, conservative, White, and male. Although this is not the group most likely to be victimized by violent criminals, it is the group most likely to be disturbed and angered by social upheaval and criminality (Butler et al., 2018; Gallup, 2023; Rancourt, 2020).

Despite the appeal of capital punishment for a slim majority of Americans, there is considerable softness to public support. There is a rather high percentage of undecideds, and public opinion has been highly unstable over time. Pollsters at the Gallup Organization have observed that "the trend of public opinion on capital punishment is among the most volatile in Gallup annals" (Gallup, 2000, p. 47). There are other signs of weakness in support for the death penalty: The public has grave doubts about whether the death penalty is fairly applied—56% of Americans believe that "Black people are more likely than White people to be sentenced to the death penalty for committing similar crimes," and 78% believe that "There is some risk that an innocent person will be put to death" (Gramlich, 2022).

Unfortunately, too many surveys have used a superficial one-question approach, and there is considerable ambiguity in the nature of the question that has typically been asked. The meaning of general support or opposition is difficult to unravel because a host of crucial questions are left unanswered by most surveys. For example, why do people support executions? Are supporters well informed about how the death penalty works? Are they aware of alternatives to capital punishment? Is there evidence of support for these alternatives?

The meaning of a response to a single survey question is uncertain. When people say that they support capital punishment, we do not know whether they mean that they favor executions for *every person* convicted of murder. We do not know if support extends to *all types* of murder (e.g., both aggravated and non-aggravated), and we do not know the *intensity* of support or opposition. Opinions expressed in response to a general survey question may indicate a mild, unstable preference or a deeply held conviction. Although there have been efforts to probe more deeply into these attitudes, it is important to remember that most discussions of public opinion begin and end with a description of general levels of support or opposition.

Some surveys have asked people to indicate reasons underlying their support or opposition. Here are the top five reasons people endorse in favor of capital punishment: "a life for a life" (35%), it saves taxpayers money (14%), they deserve it (13%), elimination of the possibility of future violence by the offender (7%), and it will deter other potential murderers (6%). Opponents of capital punishment cite the following reasons for their position: it is wrong to take a life (40%), persons may be wrongly convicted (17%), punishment should be left to God (17%), murderers will suffer longer and have more time to think about their crimes in prison (9%), and the death penalty is unfairly applied (5%) (Gallup, 2022). Over the past decade, the high cost of life imprisonment has gained the most as a reason cited for support of the death penalty. This gain has occurred despite compelling evidence that the high cost of the death penalty should instead be a reason for opposition (see Chapter 6). The possibility of wrongful conviction and executions has gained the most as a reason for opposing capital punishment.

The Dynamics of Public Opinion

There have been other significant shifts in public opinion; for example, the fading of deterrence as a justification and the ascendance of retribution ("an eye for an eye" or "a life for a life"). The move away from deterrence and toward revenge as a reason for support could be due to an awareness of research indicating no deterrent effect (see Chapter 3). But that seems somewhat unlikely given the lack of public awareness about other research findings. It seems more likely that retribution was the real motive all along, and it has simply become more socially acceptable to admit to retribution as a motivation for supporting executions.

For supporters of capital punishment, there is another benefit to the shift away from deterrence or any other pragmatic justification for capital punishment. If it is socially acceptable to support the death penalty for the sake of revenge—or some sanitized version of revenge like "a life for a life" or "retribution" or "murderers deserve to die"—then no further argument is necessary. There is no need to consider evidence on deterrence or cost or discrimination. Evidence is irrelevant. Support becomes a matter of moral conviction. We can set aside any critical, fact-based evaluation of how the death penalty actually works in the real world.

Former Supreme Court Justice Thurgood Marshall famously asserted that the utility of public opinion polls is limited because "people who were fully informed as to the purposes of the death penalty and its liabilities would find the penalty shocking, unjust, and unacceptable." Although there is some support for what has been dubbed "the Marshall Hypothesis," the effect of new information on death penalty opinions is less powerful than Marshall imagined. Some researchers have found that support is substantially eroded when people are given information about the death penalty, while others have found that only people with weak to moderate preferences are moved by facts that contradict their beliefs (Cochran, 2018). People who are strong supporters of the death penalty are much less likely to be swayed by facts. This general pattern holds for a variety of attitudes about important social issues: People whose opinions are extreme, or rooted in strong emotions or personal identity, often manage to remain unconvinced by even the most compelling evidence.

Most Americans are poorly informed about issues such as deterrence, financial costs of capital punishment, discriminatory imposition of the death penalty, and the probability of wrongful conviction. If support is based on emotion instead of reason, then asking people to endorse one or more reasons for support or opposition may not be especially informative. Some researchers have even found that people responding to surveys simply endorse every reason that potentially supports their position. That is, people who support the death penalty are likely to express a belief in deterrence, revenge, or any other justification offered them. Still, the belief in killing for the purpose of revenge is the factor that most clearly differentiates supporters from opponents. When given information challenging the effectiveness of the death penalty, those who believe most strongly in retribution show the least attitude change (Harmon et al., 2022).

The percentage of people favoring capital punishment drops precipitously when concrete rather than abstract questions are asked. When presented with summaries of three aggravated murder cases, fewer than 15% of respondents said that they would vote for the death penalty. And only a small minority of people who favor the death penalty would be willing to take an active role in its administration by being part of a jury that sentences a defendant in a capital trial or by helping to carry out an execution (Bohm, 2016). Actual imposition of a death sentence in a specific case is not something that even strong supporters of capital punishment take lightly. Consistent with these findings is the fact that real capital juries—which must be comprised of people who are willing to consider the death penalty seriously—return death sentences in only about a third of capital murder trials (McCord & Harmon, 2018; Tabak, 2022).

The unwillingness of jurors to impose the sentence of death has been interpreted as an indicator of a deep ambivalence about the penalty. As Justice William Brennan explained,

[w]hen an unusually severe punishment is authorized for wide-scale application but not, because of society's refusal, inflicted save in a few instances, the inference is compelling that there is a deep-seated reluctance to inflict it. Indeed, the likelihood is great that the punishment is tolerated only because of its disuse. (*Furman v. Georgia*, 1972)

The striking disparity between abstract approval for the death penalty and jurors' reluctance to impose it in actual cases was dramatically illustrated in the case of Nikolas Cruz. In 2022, a jury in Florida sentenced Cruz to life imprisonment without parole for the premeditated murder of seventeen people. Cruz had entered his former high school and gunned down fourteen students (aged fourteen to eighteen) as well as three staff members who were trying to help the students escape. During the planning of the attack, he had left comments on social media saying, that he was "going on a killing rampage" and that he was "going to be a professional school shooter." On the day of the mass shooting, he hid a tactical vest and weapons in a backpack and took an Uber to his former high school. He asked the driver to drop him off at a pedestrian gate that he knew would soon be open just before the school day ended.

In many ways, Cruz's crime was among the very worst of those eligible for the death penalty: fourteen children had been killed, plus three adults. There was clear evidence it was a calculated act, not an impulsive act in the heat of passion. If anyone deserved the death penalty, surely Cruz did. As the mother of one of the victims put it, "If not now the death penalty, then when?" Plus, the trial was held in Florida, one of the most pro-death penalty states in the country. Yet, despite the monstrous nature of the crime, the same jury that had convicted him decided to spare his life. At least a few of the jurors (any verdict for the death penalty would have had to be unanimous) seemed to be swayed by defense testimony that Cruz suffered from fetal alcohol syndrome caused by heavy drinking and drug use during pregnancy and that he suffered from a variety of cognitive deficits and psychological disorders. As the defense attorney put it, he was "poisoned in his mother's womb" and was "a brain damaged, broken, mentally ill person, through no fault of his own." She further argued that, "in a civilized, humane society, do we kill brain damaged, mentally ill, broken people? Do we? I hope not" (Andone et al., 2022).

One more interesting example: in 1995, at a time when violent crime rates, yearly death sentences, and the number of executions were all much higher, a jury in South Carolina sentenced Susan Smith to life imprisonment for the murder of her two young sons, Michael, aged three, and Alex, aged fourteen months. On an October evening, Smith served her sons a pizza dinner, and, like any good mother, she strapped her boys into their protective car seats before going for a drive. She drove to John Long Lake, got out of her car, shut the door, and let the car roll downhill into the dark water of the lake. A videotaped reenactment of the event suggested that the car took about six minutes to sink beneath the surface of the water. After claiming for nine days that an African American carjacker had driven off with her children, Smith confessed to committing the horrible crime.

Smith's crime was among the worst of those eligible for the death penalty: It was a double murder, both victims were helpless children, and, even worse, the killer was the very person the children relied on for love and protection. The murder was premeditated, not an impulsive act in the heat of passion. If anyone deserved the death penalty, surely Smith did. Yet, despite the monstrous nature of the crime, the same jury that had convicted her in less than three hours just as swiftly decided to spare her life. As one juror put it, "We all felt like Susan was a really disturbed person. Giving her the death penalty wouldn't serve justice" (Morganthau, 1995, p. 23). As with many capital cases, a majority of the public disagreed with the sentence. In this highly publicized case, the public had heard much of the testimony and arguments in the courtroom. Apparently, this information did not public support for executing Smith. However, even after hearing about Smith's sordid life—which included the suicide of her father and repeated sexual molestation at the hands of her stepfather—a sizable majority of the public (63%) still said that Smith should be executed. Only 28% agreed with the sentence recommended by the jury (Morganthau, 1995).

In one critical respect, the juries in the Cruz and Smith cases were like most juries in capital cases. They heard unsettling details about the twisted life of the defendant. They heard about tragically dysfunctional parents, abuse and neglect, mental disorders, and poverty. And, like most juries, they found a reason to show compassion. Although potential jurors may express abstract support for the death penalty, most actual jurors decide to spare the defendant they are called upon to judge. It is much easier to demand executions from a distance than it is to vote to kill a specific defendant.

What Drives Public Support?

In one sense, the passionate debate over capital punishment is curious: Executions have a direct effect on only a minuscule percentage of the American public. Very few Americans are murderers, victims of murderers, or friends and family of either group. Also, opinions about the death penalty are, in the main, not the product of a careful, systematic examination of relevant data. Most people know very little about our system of capital punishment. Any attempt to understand the basis of expressed support for capital punishment must take these peculiar facts into account.

One straightforward explanation is that public support for capital punishment is propelled by the rate—or, more precisely, the perceived rate—of violent crime in America. This explanation fits the data nicely: The trend line for support of the death penalty largely shadows the trend line for violent crime with a time lag. Support dropped following a period when violent crime was relatively low (i.e., the mid-1950s to late 1960s), then rose from 1968 to the early 1990s, when the violent crime rate pressed higher. The year 1968 is notable because in local and national elections, rising street crime became a major campaign theme. Support also surged after the rate of violent crime spiked in the late 1980s and early 1990s (Statistica Research, 2023). By proclaiming support for capital punishment, citizens were able to give expression to their anger and frustration about the rising tide of violence. Whenever the public perceives that little headway is being made against violent criminals, the public is willing to go farther to crack down on crime. At least in the abstract, the death penalty seems like a decisive solution to the problem of violence.

Some researchers argue that support for the death penalty is best understood as a symbolic attitude. According to this view, one's attitude toward the death penalty is a matter of self-definition and identity. The purpose is to express support for stronger methods of crime control and frustration with the apparent impotence of our criminal justice system. Symbolic attitudes reflect an underlying ideology about the importance of maintaining social order through harsh measures. Declarations of support for the death penalty appear to be driven more by emotion than cognition. They are a means of venting anger, a demand that decisive action be taken against violent criminals, and an expression of a desire to reassert social order. Support for capital punishment gives voice to both the desire for protection and the thirst for revenge.

The Shallowness of Support: Types of Murderers and Punishments

A fuller picture of the dynamics of support and opposition for the death penalty emerges when surveys ask more probing questions. For example, when asked about specific characteristics of people convicted of capital murder, opposition surges. If the defendant "endured severe physical or sexual abuse as a child," 49% oppose seeking a death sentence for the defendant (with 37% support and 14% undecided). Sixty-one percent oppose seeking death sentences against veterans who suffer from posttraumatic stress disorder, 60% oppose seeking the death penalty for "a person with a diagnosed mental illness," 63% express opposition to seeking death for people who suffer from traumatic brain injury, and 59% oppose seeking death for a person with "serious intellectual impairment" (e.g., an IQ of 75 or lower). Moreover, more people support, rather than oppose, prosecutors seeking to commute a death sentence to a sentence of life imprisonment for people with the characteristics noted above (Justice Research Group, 2022). Importantly, a substantial percentage of the people who have been sent to death row have suffered from one or more of these conditions.

Usually, voters or elected officials choose between two or more alternatives. Yet most surveys are asymmetric: They specify one alternative, the death penalty, but fail to specify the alternative punishment. Mentions of reasonable alternative punishments such as life imprisonment without the possibility of parole (LWOP) are conspicuously absent from many survey questions. Perhaps Americans are receptive to such alternatives. Maybe they would even prefer them. By asking people to choose between alternatives, it is possible to strip away some of the symbolism that accompanies the death penalty and uncover what people want in concrete, practical terms. Over the past twenty years, a series of statewide and national surveys have begun to ask people to choose among specific punishments for murderers. This simple innovation exposed deep ambivalence about use of the death penalty.

It turns out that support for capital punishment plunges when alternatives are presented. More than 10% of those who would have expressed support for capital punishment switch to LWOP when given the chance. For example, the National Crime Policy survey found that when asked whether they supported the death penalty for people convicted of murder, 74% expressed support. However, when given the choice between the death penalty and LWOP, support dropped to 53.5%

(Cullen et al., 2009). Since 2000, here are the percentages of the public endorsing LWOP as compared to the percentages of those endorsing the death penalty: In 2001, 42% versus 54%; in 2010, 46% versus 49%; and in 2019, 60% versus 36% (Gallup, 2022). Indeed, beginning in 2016, Americans have consistently favored LWOP over the death penalty.

These findings have two interesting implications: (1) Support is much weaker than commonly supposed, and (2) it appears that most Americans wrongly believe that persons convicted of capital murder are eligible for parole. That is, people don't believe that life imprisonment means that those convicted of capital murderer will never be released from prison. In states with the death penalty, the *only* alternative punishment under current law is LWOP. But few Americans realize this. It appears that the public strongly favors the death penalty only when the alternative is a prison term that allows for parole.

Concern about the possibility of parole is a pivotal consideration for an essential segment of the public: the jurors who must decide whether a defendant should be sentenced to life imprisonment or death. In post-sentencing interviews, most jurors expressed the belief that, for the defendant they judged, the actual sentence would be more lenient than the one they voted for. Specifically, jurors who voted for life imprisonment believed that the defendant would eventually be paroled, and members of juries that voted for death believed that the execution would never occur. Here are some representative quotes from members of four juries (Costanzo & Costanzo, 1994a):

- "Because of our system, the way our system is now, life imprisonment doesn't mean life imprisonment. That was a very definite factor in deciding for the death penalty."
- "Most of the people that voted for the death sentence said, Who are you kidding?. . . . Why don't you just vote for the death sentence? We know he's not going to get it. . . . We can sit here and vote for the death sentence—it doesn't mean that we're going to kill him."
- "I was convinced of it and I still am. . . . He's going to get out if you give him life imprisonment—he's going to get out. We all knew that. We talked about that. If I don't vote to kill this guy, then he's going to get out. The only way I can guarantee that he will stay in prison is to vote the death penalty."
- "If he got life imprisonment and got out in ten years or fifteen years for good behavior and goes out and does it again, how could we live with that?"

This basic finding—that jurors vastly underestimate the sentences that will be served by murderers spared the death penalty—has now been replicated with hundreds of jurors (Blume, 2010). Juries that render a death verdict often do so because they believe it is the only way to guarantee that the murderer will remain in prison for the rest of his life. Too many jurors assume that a life sentence includes parole.

Like the broader public, jurors find a life sentence without the possibility of parole appealing for a variety of reasons: It offers a good compromise between the death penalty and a life sentence in prison with parole, it achieves the goal of protecting society while avoiding the burden of responsibility for ordering the defendant's death, and it bypasses the costly and unpredictable process of appeals available to defendants sentenced to death. The comments of jurors echo the concerns of the American public. Many Americans doubt both the certainty of life imprisonment and the certainty of the death penalty. More generally, most citizens express a deep distrust of the criminal justice system and its capacity to deal effectively with violent criminals. The option of LWOP allows citizens and jurors to punish murderers severely and to protect society. At the same time, LWOP frees jurors from the heavy burden of voting to send someone to the execution chamber.

LWOP + R

Roughly half of the American public prefers LWOP, while the other half prefers the death penalty. But there is another alternative to capital punishment, one that garners the support of a clear majority of Americans: life without the possibility of parole plus restitution (LWOP + R). This sentence includes a requirement that all or part of what the convicted murderer earns from prison labor goes into a victims' support fund or is paid to the murder victim's survivors. Since 2010, in every state where LWOP + R has been offered as an alternative to the death penalty, a clear majority of survey respondents say they'd prefer it to the death penalty. For example, in North Carolina, 35% favored LWOP + R and 25% favored the death penalty (with 19% favoring LWOP). Here are the corresponding numbers for other states: Oklahoma 52% to 34% (with 14% for LWOP); Utah 47% to 29% (with 19% for LWOP); Washington 46% to 24% (with 11% for LWOP); Florida 40% to 21% (with 17% for LWOP); and Illinois 43% to 32% (with 18% for LWOP) (Allen, 2016; Capestany, 2018; Collins, 2019; Public Policy Polling, 2017). A bare majority of the American public say that they favor capital punishment for convicted murderers when the only choice is between support or opposition. But the average level of support plunges when people are asked whether they prefer LWOP or the death penalty, and support drops even farther when people are asked whether they prefer LWOP + R or the death penalty.

If LWOP + R were put into effect, prisoners serving a sentence of LWOP might be required to work, and part of what they earned from prison labor would be contributed to a victims' assistance fund. That fund could be used to provide services and to ease the financial hardships on victims' families. Obviously, neither executions nor restitution payments nor any other form of punishment can ever begin to "repay" the victims' survivors. Prisoners are typically paid very little for their labor, so for any one prisoner the amount of money contributed to a victims' fund would be small. Still, a lifetime of labor multiplied by thousands of prisoners serving life sentences could yield significant savings in the cost of incarceration and could create a significant pool of money for victims' families. By adding an element of restitution to the sentence of convicted murderers, we could show that we despise murder, but we respect human life.

It is not unrealistic to believe that the prisoners now condemned to die can be trusted to work. In some states, doomed inmates are already working as prison janitors or washing clothes in the prison laundry. For more than a decade, death-row prisoners in Texas who were classified as "work capable" made sheets, towels, uniforms, tote bags, pants, and shirts for government agencies. There was a long waiting list of prisoners who wanted to join the death row workforce, not to make money—they were paid nothing for their labor—but for the opportunity to socialize, to spend more than a couple hours a day outside their cells, and for the chance to prove that they are still capable of useful activity (Curriden, 1995).

The death penalty attracts public support because it is a symbol of severe punishment for murderers. But when we look beneath the surface, it appears that Americans have reconsidered or even embraced other harsh punishments for murderers. As the data on support for LWOP show, many people who declare support for the death penalty are simply saying that they want to make sure murderers are never allowed to walk the streets again. Such people see the death penalty as their only guarantee. Support for LWOP + R reveals that goals such as protection of society and restitution to victims may be as important as revenge and punishment. Indeed, survey data indicate that the requirement of restitution is especially appealing. What seems crucial to support for LWOP + R is the focus on protecting society and making the criminal pay. The prisoner would never again be permitted to lead a normal life, and he (or in rare cases, she) would at least be giving something back to the society he damaged.

One of the oldest debates in criminal justice has to do with striking the ideal balance among several important goals: rehabilitation of the criminal, punishment, revenge, protecting society from criminals, and restitution to victims and society at large. But which of these goals should receive the highest priority? For less serious crimes, most people would endorse a policy that emphasizes restitution over punishment—a vandal could be made to paint over graffiti or a petty thief might be made to pay for the stolen goods. But what about the most serious crime? Clearly, the response to murder must favor punishment and the protection of society. One reason the public is receptive to LWOP and LWOP + R is that both are severe forms of punishment: Murderers endure the hardships of prison for the rest of their lives before dying in prison. A second reason is that both alternatives avoid the unfair application of the death penalty that most people find troubling. More than three-quarters of Americans believe that the death penalty is arbitrary and unfair, and 38% believe the death penalty is morally wrong (Brennan, 2022). Third, both alternatives ensure that vicious murderers will never again walk outside prison walls, so society is protected. Fourth, in the case of LWOP + R, the added requirement that convicted murderers work in prison for the benefit of society enhances its appeal. It offers a vehicle for acknowledging the murder victim, and, in the optimal case, it allows for repentance.

Recent surveys demonstrate that support for the death penalty is neither as deep nor as stable as most Americans suppose. The widely cited "strong support" for the death penalty may be something of an epiphenomenon, visible only in response to a general survey question about abstract support or opposition. In declaring support for the death penalty and advocating for executions, politicians often declare that they are carrying out the will of the people. But the will of the people is weaker and differs from what many politicians presume. While citizens are not filling the streets to scream for abolition of the death penalty, the public is clearly receptive to meaningful alternative punishments. What is necessary now is for our duly elected leaders to show the courage to propose alternative punishments and to engage the public in a discussion of the real costs and illusory benefits of capital punishment. There is no doubt that violence in America is a serious problem or that murderers deserve punishment. But the death penalty does not help us solve the problem of violence. By abandoning the failed policy of killing murderers, we could expand public discourse and focus on the prevention of crime instead of the craving for revenge.

5

—————

Is the Death Penalty Cruel and Unusual?

"CRUEL AND UNUSUAL" IS AN odd legal phase. A seemingly objective term (unusual) is paired with a highly subjective term (cruel). "Unusual" typically refers to events and practices that are rare and perhaps diminishing in frequency. Determining if something is unusual appears to be largely a quantitative judgment. In contrast, cruelty is largely a qualitative judgment, and only at the extremes is there consensus about what should be considered unacceptably cruel (e.g., physical torture and slavery). One of the clearest attempts to explain the Eighth Amendment's "cruel and unusual" clause was made by Justice Brennan in *Furman v. Georgia.*

> We know "that the words of the [Clause] are not precise, and that their scope is not static." We know, therefore, that the Clause "must draw its meaning from the evolving standards of decency that mark the progress of a maturing society." That knowledge, of course, is but the beginning of the inquiry (270).
>
> At bottom, then, the Cruel and Unusual Punishments Clause prohibits the infliction of uncivilized and inhuman punishments. The State, even as it punishes, must treat its members with respect for their intrinsic worth as human beings. A punishment is "cruel and unusual," therefore, if it does not comport with human dignity (270).
>
> A punishment is excessive under this principle if it is unnecessary: the infliction of a severe punishment by the State cannot comport with human dignity when it is nothing more than the pointless infliction of

suffering. If there is a significantly less severe punishment adequate to achieve the purposes for which the punishment is inflicted, the punishment inflicted is unnecessary, and therefore excessive (279).

So, among the multiple meanings of "cruel and unusual" are that the punishment violates contemporary standards of decency, that it is inhumane because it degrades human dignity, and that it is excessive because it is unnecessary.

Early forms of execution were certainly cruel by modern standards. Stoning, drawing and quartering, and breaking at the wheel induced terrible pain and a slow, excruciating death. Sometimes the goal was to produce as much pain as possible without bringing death, for example, when the authorities wanted to secure a confession before killing the prisoner. In contrast, modern techniques typically attempt to minimize and mask the suffering of the prisoner being killed.

The three modern methods of execution most familiar to Americans—electrocution, poisonous gas, and lethal injection—were developed in, and have been mostly used in, the United States (although lethal injection is now widely used in China). Worldwide, hanging and shooting are still the most popular forms of execution. Beheading is still widespread, concentrated in Saudi Arabia and other countries influenced by Islamic law (Amnesty International, 2023a). Firing squads and scaffolds are rarely seen in the United States (although there was a shooting in 2010 and a hanging in 1996), and electric chairs and gas chambers have been abandoned. For more than a decade, lethal injection has been almost the only means of execution in the United States. As one official method of killing is replaced by another, the argument is always that the new method is more humane and respectful of human dignity. However, because of the difficulty in procuring lethal drugs and a series of botched lethal injections, some states are considering a return to execution by firing squad. It is unclear how Americans will react to the revival of this older, less sanitized form of killing. At least optically, a firing squad may seem less modern and humane than an injection.

Ropes, Bullets, Electricity, Gas, and Poison

In the early days of our country, hanging was the dominant form of execution. The goal of hanging is to snap the prisoner's spine. A noose is tightened around the neck, and a trapdoor beneath the prisoner's feet swings open. If all goes well, the cervical vertebrae are dislocated and death comes quickly. However, prior to the 1920s, even official, well-planned hangings were often botched. Despite the long drop, some prisoners failed to die from the fall and dangled from the end of the rope, slowly strangulating. Often the executioner would simply pull down on the hanging man's feet to finish the job. Even this spectacle was less gruesome than what happened when the prisoner was too heavy and the drop was too long. In such cases, the fall could rip the head from the body, leaving a bloody rope and a decapitated prisoner on the ground.

In 1942, an execution by hanging at San Quentin prison was described by the prison warden as follows:

The man hit bottom, and I observed that he was fighting by pulling on the straps, wheezing, whistling, trying to get air, blood was oozing through the Black cap. I observed also that he urinated, defecated and the droppings fell on the floor, and the stench was terrible. Several witnesses passed out and had to be carried from the witness room. Some of them threw up. It took ten minutes for the condemned man to die. When he was taken down and the cap removed, we could see that big hunks of flesh were torn off the side of his face where the noose had been, his eyes were popped, and his tongue was swollen and hanging from his mouth. His face had turned purple. (http://www.capitalpunishmentuk.org/hanging.html)

Death by hanging has always had its enthusiasts. One early scholar put it like this, "No one can point to a method which is more beautiful and expeditious, or which is aesthetically superior to the practice of breaking their necks by hanging" (Duff, 1961, p. 5). Indeed, modern hangings in the United States seldom go awry. Hanging is now a precise, scientific (though somewhat ghoulish) procedure: The prisoner is carefully weighed and measured, the rope is stretched and waxed to prevent springing or coiling, the optimal length of necessary drop is carefully calculated for the weight of the condemned man, and the execution routine is well rehearsed by prison personnel. However, even if the hanged man has lost consciousness, the body may briefly convulse. That spectacle is disturbing to many witnesses.

Execution by firing squad can bring death by massive damage to internal organs, or damage to the central nervous system, or by hemorrhage. The 1996 execution of John Taylor in Utah provides a glimpse into the modern method of death by shooting (Taylor claimed he was innocent and chose a firing squad over lethal injection to embarrass state officials). Taylor was strapped into a wooden armchair and a hood was placed over his head. A stethoscope was used to locate his heart and a red cloth target was pinned to the site. Five anonymous sharpshooters fired on command and Taylor died quickly. A large pan was positioned under his chair to collect the draining blood. A state official reported that in the thirty-nine executions by firing squad he had witnessed, it had taken anywhere from fifteen seconds to twenty-seven minutes for the prisoner to die (Sahagun, 1996).

In 1879, Thomas Edison invented the electric lightbulb, and, ten years later, a condemned prisoner was electrocuted in New York. The electric chair was intended to replace the noose because killing by electrocution was thought to be more humane, modern, and scientific. A mysterious, invisible force would simply be passed through the prisoner's body and he would expire almost instantly. It was to be a quiet, tidy form of killing. Edison opposed capital punishment and did not want to see his "direct current" associated with killing. He recommended use of the "alternating current" advocated by his rival George Westinghouse on the grounds that it was "more dangerous" (Cline, 2017). In 1890, William Kemmler became the first person to be strapped to the electric chair and electrocuted. At first, the execution seemed to be going smoothly. But after about seventeen seconds of electrocution, the current failed. A few moments later, Kemmler's chest "began to heave" and he moaned and gasped for air. A much stronger charge was then delivered for about two minutes. Witnesses reported smoke rising from Kemmler's head accompanied by the smell of burning flesh. The most recent use of the electric chair was in Alabama, in 2022, when Lynda Lyon Block was killed for killing a police officer.

To prepare for electrocution, part of a prisoner's leg and head are shaved to afford good contact with electrodes. On the fateful day, the prisoner is strapped to the chair and a powerful surge of electricity (about 1,900 volts) is passed through his body. Although the official goal is paralysis of the heart and respiratory system due to burning of the internal organs, "the condemned prisoner often leaps forward against restraining straps when the switch is thrown; the prisoner may defecate, urinate, or vomit blood. Eyewitnesses often report that there is a smell of burned flesh" (Amnesty International, 1989).

In the case of lethal gas, the prisoner is strapped to a steel chair in an airtight chamber with a stethoscope taped to the chest. The heartbeat can be monitored from an adjacent room and is used to fix the time of death. A lever outside of the death chamber is pulled to drop capsules of sodium cyanide into a vat of sulfuric acid. Cyanide gas fills the chamber, and death is caused by "asphyxiation due to inhibition by the cyanide gas of the respiratory enzymes which transfer oxygen from the blood to the body cells" (Amnesty International, 1989, p.60). A sort of cellular suffocation.

Lethal injection is the most recent innovation in the technology of execution. First tried in Texas, in 1982, it is now the most widely used technique in the United States. The prisoner is strapped to a gurney on his back, and needles that will deliver the poison are inserted in both arms, usually just opposite the elbow. Usually, three substances are injected: the first is a fast-acting anesthetic, the second is a drug that paralyzes the diaphragm and respiratory muscles, and the third drug stops the heart. However, some states have moved to a two-drug or even a one-drug procedure (pentobarbital or sodium thiopental).

China is the only other country to widely use lethal injection. Other countries have considered and rejected the technique for various reasons. For example, before Great Britian abolished the death penalty, the Royal Commission on Capital Punishment carefully explored the possibility of using lethal injection. The commission reached the conclusion that lethal injection did not provide "reasonable certainty" that a prisoner would be killed "quickly, painlessly, and decently in all cases." Among the problems identified were that some prisoners did not have easily accessible veins, that all drugs would need to be effective and properly combined, and that the executioner would need to have significant medical skill (Denno, 2018). Despite such concerns, several states in the United States advocated for a switch to lethal injections. The advantages seemed compelling: It was far cheaper than gas chambers or electric chairs; and, compared to an electrocution or gassing, anyone viewing a lethal injection would see much less suffering and struggle by the condemned man (this was especially important because there was considerable discussion of televising executions at the time). As one legislator (who had no medical training) put it, lethal injection would produce "no pain, no spasms, no smells or sound—just sleep, then death" (Denno, 2007, p. 67). These perceived benefits made the new technique far more palatable to state legislatures and governors.

Are any of these techniques of killing truly humane? It is impossible to know. Almost no one gets out of the execution chamber alive. In 1946, because of a malfunction in the machinery of death, seventeen-year-old

Willie Francis experienced a few seconds of electrocution and lived to tell about it. He said the experience was extremely painful, and that "my mouth tasted like cold peanut butter. I felt a burning in my head and my left leg, and I jumped against the straps. I saw little blue and pink and green speckles" (King, 2009). A year later, Francis had his second date with the executioner. The Supreme Court was unpersuaded by his argument that it was "cruel and unusual" to execute him twice. On the second try, the execution went according to plan.

Although each of the five methods described above has been touted as especially civilized and humane at some point in history, no method works perfectly on every occasion. As noted earlier, botched hangings sometimes led to decapitation or slow strangulation. In the case of a firing squad, nervous shooters may not hit the intended target. In 1951, a prisoner named Elisio Mares faced a firing squad. Mares was well-liked by the prison staff, and when the command to shoot came, all five sharpshooters aimed away from his heart. The bullets tore through the right side of his chest, leaving Mares to bleed to death slowly. As the British Royal Commission on Capital Punishment noted more than seventy years ago, execution by firing squad, "does not possess even the first requisite of an efficient method, the certainty of causing immediate death" (Royal Commission, 1953, p. 154).

Modern American techniques—electrocution, poisonous gas, and lethal injection—are not without problems of their own. Botched executions can be the result of mistakes by the executioners, equipment problems, or struggling by the condemned prisoner. In 1985, Alpha Otis Stephens was strapped to the electric chair in Georgia. Stephens had to be hit with three separate 1,900-volt surges of electricity. After the first surge he "struggled for breath for eight minutes." When the second surge was applied, "his body slumped when the current stopped . . . but shortly afterward witnesses saw him struggle to breathe. In the six minutes allowed for the body to cool before it could be examined, Mr. Stephens took 23 breaths" (Amnesty International, 1995). When the doctors declared that he was still alive, a third jolt finished him off ten minutes later. His experience was not unique. Also in 1985, William Vandiver needed five separate charges of electricity and seventeen minutes to die. And, in 1990, "flames, smoke and sparks shot six inches out of the head of Jessie Tafero as three 2,000-volt shocks were administered. Because the amperage was incorrect, Tafero's flesh cooked on his bones before he died" (Trombley, 1992, p. 14). And, in 1991, mistakes by the execution team led to a hideous spectacle in the execution of Albert

Clozza. "Steam pressure in Clozza's head caused his eyeballs to pop so that blood ran down his chest from the sockets" (Trombley, 1992, p. 14). According to Fred Leuchter, a major designer of execution machinery, the problem with electrocution is that,

> if you overload an individual's body with current . . . you'll cook the meat on his body. It's like meat on an overcooked chicken. If you grab the arm, the flesh will fall right off in your hands. That doesn't mean he felt anything. It simply means that it's cosmetically not the thing to do. Presumably the state will return the remains to the victim's family for burial. Returning someone who had been cooked would be in poor taste. (Brandon, 1999, p. 248)

Once considered a humane alternative to electrocution, lethal gas has slowly been almost abandoned. As prisoners succumb to the effects of poisonous gas, most buck and strain against the restraining straps, and many convulse for several minutes before finally dying. In a 1995 lawsuit alleging that gassing was unnecessarily cruel, a physician testified that "veterinarians won't even use cyanide to put dogs to sleep" (Newsweek, 1995).

There now appears to be a consensus that lethal injection is the most humane—or at least the most humane-looking—method of killing. Based on external indicators of pain and distress (i.e., screaming, sweating, facial grimaces, defecation, and urination, vomiting, pupil dilation, writhing of the body), one neurobiologist concluded that injection probably causes the least suffering (Hillman, 1993). However, such signs are imperfect indicators of pain since leather restraints and the effects of muscle relaxants suppress movements of the face and body. After more than forty years of using lethal injection, one scholar has observed that, "the methods for euthanizing animals require substantially more medical consultation and concern for humaneness than the techniques used to execute human beings" (Denno, 2018).

Most states that authorize the death penalty now list lethal injection as their primary form of execution. South Carolina is the lone exception. In 2021, because of the difficulty in obtaining the deadly drugs required for lethal injection, the South Carolina legislature voted to switch to firing squads or electrocution. Oklahoma now allows for electrocution or firing squad as alternative methods if legal injection is eventually ruled unconstitutional.

Sometimes, the injection of deadly chemicals goes smoothly—no violent convulsing of the body, no mutilated corpse. Yet there are problems with even this most sanitized form of execution. If the prisoner has a history of intravenous drug use, the executioner may have to use minor surgery to locate a suitable deep vein. If the prisoner struggles for his life, insertion of the needle can be difficult and painful. In 2022, Kenneth Smith remained strapped to the execution gurney for more than three hours. The execution team repeatedly jabbed his arms, hands, and collarbone area in a failed attempt to find a vein for delivering the lethal drugs. The execution was halted just before midnight because the execution warrant was about to expire. When he was unstrapped from the gurney, he was "trembling, sweating, hyperventilating, dizzy, and could not lift his own arms to be handcuffed, or walk unassisted" (Pilkington, 2022). Technical problems are also possible. The lethal drugs can be improperly combined, the drugs may thicken and clog the delivery tube or needle, and/or the anesthetic may not take effect immediately.

In 2021, John Grant was executed by lethal injection in Oklahoma. After receiving the first drug of three drugs (midazolam), "Grant's body shook and jerked nearly two dozen times before vomit spurted from his mouth and spilled down his neck" (Peiser & Armario, 2021). An autopsy of his body found "pulmonary edema"—a buildup of fluid in the lungs that produces a sensation of drowning. This fluid buildup in the lungs has been found in 76–84% of the autopsies of inmates who have been executed by lethal injection and likely explains the gasping for air and straining against the straps observed during many executions (Caldwell et al., 2020; Zivot et al., 2022). All the drug combinations that have been used in lethal injections can produce pulmonary edema, which is especially likely when the drugs are used in high doses and administered quickly. In federal court, one coroner opined that a prisoner being killed by lethal injection, "would experience severe respiratory distress with associated sensations of drowning, asphyxiation, panic and terror" (In re: Ohio, 2019, p. 70).

Lethal injection also allows for a more insidious type of botched execution: a painful, lingering death that *appears* to be painless and swift. When injecting the lethal drugs, "even a small error in dosage or administration can leave a prisoner conscious but paralyzed while dying—a sentient witness of his or her own slow, lingering asphyxiation" (*Chaney v. Heckler*, 1983, p. 1177). Medical researchers have concluded that "Instead of falling off to sleep and dying," many condemned men were "drowning in their own secretions and suffocating to death, sometimes masked by a paralytic" (Smith, 2022).

By 2007, every state with the death penalty listed lethal injection as the sole or secondary method of execution. A few states offered condemned inmates a second choice of being killed by electrocution, hanging, or firing squad. However, legal challenges to execution protocols in several states asserted that lethal injection violated the Eighth Amendment's ban on "cruel and unusual punishments." The Supreme Court reviewed these challenges in the Kentucky case of *Baze v. Rees* in 2008. In a 7–2 decision, the Court upheld the constitutionality of the lethal injection, finding that the commonly used three-drug protocol did not constitute "wanton exposure to objectively intolerable risk of serious harm" when compared to known and available alternatives.

A mere seven years later, in *Glossip v. Gross*, in 2015, the Supreme Court held in a 5–4 decision that using the drug midazolam as a substitute for sodium thiopental did not create "a substantial risk of severe pain." The substitution of the drug was made necessary because the lone remaining US manufacturer of sodium thiopental stopped manufacturing it, and European drug suppliers refused to sell any barbiturate to state corrections departments. Shortages of the drugs needed for lethal injection are ongoing. Attempts to import the necessary drugs from other countries (e.g., India) have been disallowed because they do not meet standards set by the US Food and Drug Administration (FDA), and several pharmaceutical companies have expressed concerns about the financial and reputational impact of producing drugs for execution chambers. Some companies have enforced restrictions on their drugs to prevent their use in lethal injections.

The difficulty of obtaining lethal drugs and the increasing frequency of botched executions have led some states to announce that they might return to firing squads or a new form of killing—nitrogen hypoxia—which suffocates the condemned prisoner using nitrogen gas. To deliver the gas, a specially designed death mask has been created. Ideally, the death mask prevents the lethal gas from leaking out while simultaneously preventing life-giving oxygen from being sucked in by the condemned prisoner. Cells and organs are starved of the oxygen vital to their functioning and eventually the heart stops (Smith, 2022). The amount of pain produced by this new procedure—a procedure which was proposed by politicians, not scientists or medical professionals—is not known. In 2024, Alabama became the first state to kill a prisoner using the new method. Although state officials had predicted that condemned man—Kenneth Smith—would be rendered unconscious in a few seconds, witnesses reported that Smith appeared to remain conscious for several minutes, that he "writhed and convulsed on the gurney," and struggled against his restraints (Czachor, 2024; Pilkington, 2024).

Because lethal injection seemed to be the most humane way of killing prisoners, even many opponents of capital punishment came to favor the needle over the rope, the bullet, the electric chair, and the gas chamber. But the switch to the syringe had the unintended consequence of making executions seem almost civilized. A prisoner lying faceup on a hospital gurney is subjected to what looks like a routine medical procedure. The only difference is that the goal is to kill instead of heal.

In the distant past, executions were savage spectacles. Modern American techniques mute this savagery, although the occasional botched execution still calls up associations with the barbaric rituals of the past. And, if no drug-based, pseudo-medical procedure can be developed to get around the shortage of lethal drugs and the lack of medically trained execution personnel, states may be forced to return to past techniques like firing squads and hanging. The problem is that death by firing squad or hanging *seems* more like killing. Maybe killing by the state can be made swift, simple, sanitized, and perhaps more humane. But, from the perspective of politicians and proponents of the death penalty, the essential thing is to develop a method of killing that does not arouse doubts or revulsion in American public. Politically, the best method is the one that will anesthetize the public conscience along with the condemned man.

Between Sentencing and Execution: Life on Death Row

Death rows are prisons within prisons. Located inside the maximum-security units of state penitentiaries, they are segregated from the general prison population. Death rows are special areas of the prison designed to hold inmates who are waiting to be killed. In many ways, death row is little more than a warehouse, a storage facility for people awaiting their appointment with the executioner. Because it is assumed that few inmates will get out of death row alive, there is no attempt to educate, rehabilitate, or in any way improve the residents of the row. With few exceptions, there is no access to training programs or prison work. The conditions of confinement are even more restrictive than those for the general prison population. In most states, the inhabitants of death row spend about twenty-two hours per day in their cells. For a couple of hours each day, they are free to play games and roam a concrete yard bounded by fences and razor wire. Here is how one inmate described it:

> When the shift changes at 6:00 AM, a guard comes around to take a list of those who want to go out to the dog kennel run like exercise yards that I can go to five days a week for two hours a day. The two days a week that I do not get an opportunity to go to the yard I am confined to the cell for 24 hours. There is no shelter in the yard so on rainy or snow days I am confined to the cell for many days straight without even a brief relief. (Johnson, 2018, p. 590)

Most death-row inmates spend about twenty-one hours a day in a seven-by-ten-foot cell. Here is how one resident of death row described his cell:

> I'm in a single person cell. The cell is literally all concrete and steel. The bed I was sleeping on is a concrete slab with a thin mattress on it. The walls are cinderblocks three quarters of the way around, but the front of the cell is a wall of steel bars. . . . The toilet is right next to the bed and built into the back wall. The toilet and sink are a single unit of brushed steel. There is a metal cabinet affixed to the wall at the front of the cell for personal property and there is a cement table right beside it for me to put my food tray on. A plastic chair completes the furnishings of the cell. (Johnson, 2018, p. 589)

If you tore out the bathtub in your family bathroom and replaced it with a bed, you would probably have something a bit nicer than an average cell on death row. Imagine spending the next ten years of your life in your reconstructed bathroom. Each day you have twenty-four hours to fill; each week you have 168 hours. Even if you eat your meals very slowly and sleep ten hours per day, there are still hundreds of days and thousands of hours to fill each year. The idleness, monotony, and relentless boredom are enough to unravel the sanity of most death row inmates. The one commodity death-row inmates have in abundance is time. Their constant enemies are crushing boredom and loss of all hope. There is too much time to think and little to think about. As one observer noted, "The inhabitants of the row live lives that don't bear much thinking about. There's the ugly past that got them to this place, the miserable present, and the future they don't want to come" (Von Drehle, 1995, p. 3).

Three times a day, the occupants of death row receive a meal through a slot in their cell door. A few days a week they are locked into a metal cage with a shower head for a timed shower. Perhaps two or three hours a day they are permitted to go outdoors to a fenced-in concrete area known as "the yard." At night the lights in the cells are dimmed, but the lights in the corridor still burn brightly. Ventilation is poor, and the air is stagnant and full of the smells of men who seldom shower as well as the smells from scores of toilets. It is usually too hot in summer, too cold in winter, and it is almost always noisy. Men yell to one another through the bars, televisions play, rolling carts clatter through the corridors, steel doors slam shut. Sometimes the voices of inmates suffering from psychological deterioration are added to the cacophony.

> I am in an area now where one of the men is seriously mentally ill. He talks to himself all day and late into the night. Often, he screams that he is being raped and acts out the drama over and over again. (Johnson, 2019, p. 86)

Another factor that shapes life on death row is the interest in maintaining security. Of course, all prison administrators have strong concerns about security, but these concerns are magnified on death row. The correctional officers responsible for carrying out the elaborate security procedures on death row feel especially vulnerable to attack. As one noted,

> They [the prisoners] will hurt you to get away. You've got to watch them all the time. You know if these guys get a chance, you're gone. They'll kill you. They've all killed before. There was always that thought in my mind. I feel they don't have anything to lose. (Johnson, 2018, p. 592)

Such worries may be overblown, but if a prisoner were able to smuggle in a weapon, the results could be disastrous. Prison workers are fond of telling stories about ingenious attempts to smuggle in contraband. Two different prison workers told me that one prisoner's girlfriend swallowed a small balloon filled with drugs just prior to her visit. Once in the visiting room, she managed to regurgitate the balloon and pass it into the mouth of the prisoner by means of a kiss. According to the guards, the prisoner then swallowed the balloon and later retrieved the drugs from his own feces.

Because of security concerns, visitors must pass through a metal detector and undergo a thorough search. Security is also the official reason for the policy of "noncontact visits" in some death rows. Though security is the rationale for prohibiting contact, the effect is to further isolate the prisoner from his loved ones. The noted psychiatrist Karl Menninger called the noncontact visit needlessly cruel and "a violation of ordinary principles of humanity." Here is an account of a noncontact visit between an inmate and his young daughter.

> She burst into the tiny visiting room, her brown eyes aglitter with happiness; stopped, stunned, staring at the glassy barrier between us; and burst into tears. . . . In milliseconds, sadness and shock shifted into fury as her petite fingers curled into tight fists, which banged and pummeled the Plexiglas barrier, which shuddered and shimmied but didn't shatter. "Break it! Break it!" she screamed. Her mother, recovering from her shock, bundled up my daughter in her arms, as sobs rocked them both. . . . "Why can't I hug him? Why can't we kiss? Why can't I sit in his lap? Why can't we touch? Why not?" (Abu-Jamal, 1995, p. 26)

Many, if not most, death row inmates slowly lose their ties to the outside world. The families of the inmates—who are uniformly poor—often cannot afford to miss work or spend the money to make the long trip to prisons that are located far from population centers. Visits are difficult and painful for most loved ones, and, over a period of years, visitors arrive far less often or not at all. And there are greatly diminished opportunities to form relationships with guards or other inmates. Guards assigned to death row "shall avoid any personal discussions," instructs a manual for death row staffers. "Employees must not be too familiar or discuss personal items of interest with the inmates" (Johnson, 2005, p. 44).

Social scientists and death row inmates have long attempted to identify the essential features of life on death row: loss of control over all aspects of life, an almost total loss of privacy, loneliness, isolation, crushing boredom, enforced idleness, vulnerability to prison staff and other inmates. Although these are features of prison life in general, pain and privation are amplified on the row. Visits are less frequent and more restrictive, opportunities for work or education range from none to few, there is far less out-of-cell time, there are few opportunities to form friendships, and, most important, there is the agonizing knowledge that the state intends to kill you.

Waiting for the Executioner

Just prior to his retirement from the Supreme Court, Justice Harry Blackmun declared his opposition to capital punishment. He described lethal injection in graphic terms: "Intravenous tubes attached to his arms will carry the instrument of death, a toxic fluid designed specifically for the purpose of killing human beings." Justice Antonin Scalia countered by recounting the brutal rape and murder of an eleven-year-old: "How enviable a quiet death by lethal injection compared with that!" he wrote (*Callins v. Collins*, 1994, p. 127). And, of course, he is right. Compared to most capital murders, the state's killing seems clean and humane. Even the most efficient murder—a bullet that rips through the chest or the head— seems more brutal than a meticulously planned killing carried out by the state. But an execution can only be considered humane if we confine our view to the act of execution. It is the cruel preliminaries that produce the most pain. As Albert Camus put it,

> [f]or there to be equivalence, the death penalty would have to punish a criminal who had warned his victim of the date at which he would inflict a horrible death on him and who, from that moment onward, had confined him at his mercy for months. Such a monster is not encountered in private life. (Camus, 1960, p. 199)

The moment of execution is only the final moment in a long process that begins with sentencing. Once the death sentence is pronounced, the prisoner knows that he will die in prison—either he will be killed there, or he will die there of natural causes. Because of the possibilities of a new trial, or a successful appeal, or a commuted sentence, the moods of death row inmates are likely to swing between mild hope and abject despair.

Death row inmates are tormented by intrusive thoughts about their impending execution. They imagine how they will behave in the hours and minutes leading up to their death, they speculate about the pain of being executed, they wonder if their legs will collapse under them as they walk to the death chamber. Many are haunted by recurring nightmares about their execution, and about 70% suffer from severe depression and symptoms of psychosis. As one death row inmate explained,

> I sit in that cell, you know, and it seems like I'm just ready to scream or go crazy or something. . . . I sit up at night, you know. You just sit there,

and it seems like things are closing in on you. Like last night, when I sit in there and everything's real quiet, just a buzzing noise gets going in my ears. And I sit there, and I consciously think, "Am I going crazy?" And the buzzing gets louder; and you sit there and you want to scream. (Johnson, 2019, p. 49)

Condemned men also ruminate about how the execution and the publicity surrounding it will affect their fathers, mothers, spouses, siblings, and children. A psychiatrist who worked with the condemned concluded that confinement on death row,

> invariably results in claustrophobia, and often results in chronic anxiety and depression. Prisoners eventually lose the will to live. The prolonged confinement in a small cell with a light kept burning by night could be regarded as a form of psychological torture. (Leahy et al., 2003, p. 161)

If torture, as defined by the United Nations, consists of "severe pain or suffering, whether physical or mental," then waiting for years or decades for an appointment with the executioner surely qualifies as psychological torture. According to the testimonies of torture survivors around the world, "The threat of execution is one of the most terrifying forms of torture" (Amnesty International, 2023b). To make the abstract threat real, occasionally a fellow resident of the row is taken from his cell and escorted to the execution chamber. Here is how one death row inmate put it:

> The courts give you an execution date, that's true. But you don't know what's going to take place between then and your execution date. You don't know when you're going to be moved to the silent cell over there. That's right down the hall, what they call a waiting cell. You don't know when you're going to be moved down there. And this keeps you jumpy, and it keeps you nervous, and it keeps you scared. (Johnson, 2018, p. 590)

Indeed, many condemned prisoners become so despondent that they decide to abandon further appeals and ask the state to carry out the execution. They submit to a sort of state-sponsored suicide. Death starts to seem like the only way to escape their miserable existence.

Being sentenced to death is a quadruple punishment—there are the standard pains of long imprisonment, there are the special pains of near solitary confinement for a period of years or decades, there is the suffering of waiting for the agents of the state to kill you, and, finally, there is the execution itself.

The Execution Ritual

For nearly all Americans, the death penalty is an abstract topic of debate. But even Americans who support it don't really want to be bothered by the details. An execution is a personal, real event for only a few prison workers, a few witnesses, and the prisoner being killed. Some prison workers claim to be unmoved by executions. One member of an "execution team" dismissed the stress of his job.

> I can take or leave executions. It's not a job I like or dislike. It's a job I've been asked to do. . . . If they would stop the death penalty, it wouldn't bother me. If we had ten executions tomorrow, it wouldn't bother me. I would condition my mind to get me through it. (Johnson, 2019, p. 67)

Every step in the execution process, from the issuing of the death warrant to the time when the corpse is carried out of the death chamber, is spelled out in meticulous detail. Twenty-four hours prior to the execution, the prisoner is moved to a special cell next to the chamber, two guards are posted outside the cell to prevent the prisoner from committing suicide and "to move him through a series of critical and cumulatively demoralizing junctures beginning with his last meal and ending with his last walk" (Johnson, 2019, p. 68). This is the "deathwatch." There is a final visit with loved ones, the prisoner is served his last meal, his meager personal possessions are boxed for distribution to relatives after the execution, a "spiritual adviser" is allowed to visit, a final shower is taken, the prisoner is dressed in a clean execution uniform, a photograph is taken, the death warrant is read aloud. If death is to be caused by electrocution, the head and leg are shaved to ensure good contact with the electrodes; if poisonous gas is to be used, cyanide capsules are bagged in cheesecloth so that they can be lowered into the bowl of acid; and if the killing is to be accomplished by lethal injection, several syringes are prepared.

Each member of the "execution team"—the prison officials who prepare for and carry out the execution—has a specific and limited duty: to watch the prisoner for a six-hour shift, to escort the prisoner on his final walk to the chamber, to tighten one or more of the leather straps that hold the prisoner to a chair or gurney. Responsibility for the killing is diffused among several members of the team. According to one commentator, the bureaucratic ritual leading up to the moment of execution,

> arose as a necessary device to keep order in the prison around the time of an execution, to keep the execution party's mind off the grisliness of their task over a period as long as ten days, and to control the condemned man's fear by making him believe he was a part of a ritual that was being conducted in a competent way by well-trained people. (Trombley, 1992, p. 19)

In his moving books, *Death Work* and *Condemned to Die*, the great scholar of death row, Robert Johnson, notes that very few condemned prisoners must be forcibly dragged to the execution chamber. Condemned men have already been tamed and exhausted by years of confinement. Something resembling emotional death has already been accomplished and all that remains is to kill the body. "The officials' goal, and in the end perhaps the prisoner's as well, is a smooth, orderly, and ostensibly voluntary execution, one that looks humane and dignified and is not sullied in any way by obvious violence" (Johnson, 2005, p. 84). To win the cooperation of the prisoner, guards help him through the ritual, attend to his needs, and try to keep his mind off the impending execution. And "the prisoner, obviously in distress, is admonished to walk to his death like a man. In conformity with the official script, the executioners, in control of themselves and the situation, imply that, in exchange, they will do the job cleanly and without a hitch." As one official put it, "I seen most of them right there at the end. They weaken to the point where they'll be almost crying, and I tell them, I say, 'Well, you don't want to go out like that.' I say, 'People be here in a minute—pull yourself up.'... That works every time for me" (Johnson, 2005, p. 97).

The people responsible for the execution must not only try to induce the prisoner to meet his death without resistance or incident, they must also psychologically prepare themselves for their grim task. Johnson found that members of the execution team prepared themselves by thinking about the horrible crime committed by the condemned man. As one prison officer put it, "You read the papers and things, and you brush up on the case and just see what this man has done, you know . . . you try to find out all the dirty things that he done. So, you say, 'Well, okay, it's okay. It's all right, all right to put him to death" (Johnson, 2005, p. 107).

Despite their efforts to carry out executions without suffering lingering effects, members of execution teams seldom emerge unscathed by their experiences. In a letter to the governor of Arkansas, twenty-three former corrections officials argued that,

> [t]here is absolutely no way to conduct a well-run execution without causing at least one person to lose a little bit of their humanity, or to start at least one person on the cumulative path to post-traumatic stress. (Pilkington, 2017, p. 3)

One warden who oversaw executions came to feel that they were not morally acceptable. He concluded that, "Being a correctional Officer is supposed to be an honorable profession. The state dishonors us by putting us in this situation. This is premeditated, carefully thought-out ceremonial killing" (Timmins, 2010).

The rules and procedures designed, in part, to prevent the prison staff from feeling sympathy for condemned inmates sometimes fail. Those assigned to carry out executions are sometimes deeply affected by the experience. Donald Cabana, a former prison warden, described an execution he presided over as the most difficult experience of his life. He also described the burden placed on other prison workers.

> I watched the terrible pain of guards who had worked for eight years with this young man and who would turn their face from you, not in shame, but because they didn't want you to see the emotions and the pain and the burden on them. I could see the stress and pressure that was bearing down on all of them. (Cabana, 1998, p. 199)

Cabana writes that prison officials believe that "people can and do change" and that most people do, such as the man described below:

> this young Black man arrived on death row as an 18-year-old who was embittered, a drug addict, and feeling sorry for himself. The young man I was going to be asked to execute was so very different. He was at peace

with himself, he was at peace with the world, and he was at peace with his God. . . . I had watched a human being change before my eyes over the course of eight years, a person who had become a different and far better person, in many respects far better than me or than many people I knew. (Cabana, 1998, p. 196)

The burden and strain of carrying out a death sentence reaches beyond prison personnel, the family of the victim, and the family of the condemned. It is also felt by investigators, police officers, prosecuting attorneys, defense attorneys, jurors, and judges, all of whom must devote considerable time and effort either to block or to clear the way for an execution. The emotional toll can be heavy. Even journalists who witness the execution report some short-term symptoms of stress, including crying, listlessness, inability to concentrate, and nightmares (Freinkel et al., 1994).

Because the first principle of medical ethics is "Do no harm," the involvement of medical personnel in executions is a fundamental breach of medical ethics. In response to protests by medical associations, some states have passed laws designed to circumvent the prohibitions of those associations. To entice medical professionals into the process of killing, states have guaranteed that they will conceal their identities and pay them in cash. In Georgia, a law was written to stipulate that physicians who assist with executions are not technically practicing medicine so, therefore, they cannot be disciplined by medical associations. Such laws are vigorously opposed by national medical associations (e.g., the American Medical Association, the American Association for the Advancement of Science, the American College of Physicians, the American Public Health Association, and Physicians for Human Rights) (Henry, 2018). Even the limited role of having a physician "pronounce death" poses a fundamental ethical dilemma. Inevitably, some people have not yet expired when the physician is called in to pronounce death. The physician must then signal the executioner to continue electrocuting, gassing, or injecting.

The existence of the death penalty makes other medical grotesqueries necessary. No condemned man is allowed to cheat the executioner by committing suicide. Indeed, if the man is physically sick or insane, medical professionals must restore him to health before they turn him over to the executioner. Hours before his scheduled execution in 1995, death row inmate Robert Beecher managed to take an overdose of sedatives in an apparent suicide attempt. He was rushed to the hospital where his stomach was pumped, and, once he fully regained consciousness, he was strapped to a gurney and killed by lethal injection. His execution was delayed only two hours. In 2018, Alabama executed eighty-three-year-old Walter Moody and had scheduled the execution of sixty-seven-year-old Vernon Madison. Madison was incontinent, unable to walk without assistance, legally blind, and had experienced several strokes that wiped away his memory of the crimes that sent him to death row. He died shortly before he could be sent to the execution chamber. In 1991, Donald Gaskin tried to end his life by slashing his wrists and elbows, but only succeeded in passing out from loss of blood. A physician was called in to stitch up the wounds and Gaskin was strapped to a gurney in his cell. When he regained consciousness, he was escorted to the electric chair.

Laws in many states require that the condemned prisoner must be fully aware of his execution and the reasons for it. This means that psychologists and other mental health professionals are also put in an ethical bind. Their testimony at trial about the mental capacity and competence of a capital defendant may lead to a death sentence. And once a death sentence is handed down, other mental health professionals may be asked to certify that the condemned prisoner is competent to be executed.

Cruelty from a Safe Distance

We can demand that murderers be killed, but few of us would want to do the killing. Many Americans support the death penalty in the abstract, but few juries are willing to impose it when faced with a living, breathing, though vicious and deeply flawed, human being. We simply want the government to take care of it, cleanly and efficiently, in a distant prison, away from public view. Yet by demanding that killers be killed, we place a great burden on jurors, lawyers, judges, prison officials, the families of condemned men, and even on the families of victims. More and more people are pulled into the circle of suffering. By demanding an eye for an eye, we create the necessity for death rows where the conditions of confinement and waiting for death amount to a form of slow torture. The threat of execution slowly steals away the sanity of many, if not most, condemned men.

You may feel that it is morally acceptable to kill murderers. But is it morally acceptable to subject them to psychological torture before we kill them? And, most important, what does it say about us and our society? As many moral scholars have noted, the morality of a society is judged not by how it treats its best citizens, but by how it treats its worst criminals.

6

Is the Death Penalty Cheaper Than
Life Imprisonment?

DISAGREEMENTS ABOUT THE DEATH PENALTY usually turn on issues of fairness, morality, and effectiveness. But there is also the question of money. Although a purely economic analysis might be considered vulgar or irrelevant to discussion of a life-or-death issue, assertions about financial cost often emerge in debates about the value of the death penalty.

Proponents of capital punishment sometimes claim that killing murderers saves the money of overburdened taxpayers. Some Americans say they support capital punishment because they believe it is cheaper to execute a condemned prisoner than to imprison that person for the remainder of his or her natural life. Depending on the year, public opinion surveys show that between 11% and 20% of Americans support the death penalty, in part, because they believe it "saves taxpayers money" (Gallup, 2022). Surprisingly, saving money is the second most important justification for those who support capital punishment (the first is retribution— "an eye for an eye"). Questions of cost even surface when jurors are deciding whether to sentence a particular defendant to death. As one juror in a capital murder trial put it, "Why should the taxpayers have to pay to keep this guy alive in prison for the rest of his life?" (Costanzo & Costanzo, 1994b).

On its face, this belief seems reasonable—surely by killing condemned prisoners we save years or even decades of costs associated with room and board. Prison is expensive, and a young murderer could live for decades after conviction. Yet, despite the intuitive appeal of the cheaper-to-execute notion, it is mistaken.

In centuries past, people found guilty of hanging crimes were escorted to the gallows within days of being convicted. Reckoning was swift and cheap. The cost of the death penalty was a modest fee paid to the executioner plus the cost of erecting a scaffold. But things have changed. As American society evolved, our system of capital punishment has been reshaped by concerns about fairness, consistency, morality, and the possibility of wrongful conviction. As a result, the death penalty is no longer swift or cheap.

The Price Tag

To be sure, the cost of life imprisonment without parole (LWOP)—the only alternative to a death sentence—is very high. A full accounting of the cost of LWOP must include the maintenance and operational costs of a maximum-security cell as well as the costs of healthcare, food, and security personnel. These costs typically continue to accrue for years or decades. Given the high price of imprisonment, it is possible to imagine an individual case where an execution might be less expensive than life imprisonment. Consider the case of a healthy nineteen-year-old convicted of first-degree murder. If he is sentenced to death, refuses to appeal his sentence, and is executed ten years later, it *may* end up being cheaper than if he had been sentenced to LWOP and died of natural causes fifty years later. But such hypothetical cases miss the point: Cost estimates must include the cost of financing our system of capital punishment. It is not just the cost of a particular case that is relevant—it is the full cost of sustaining an elaborate death-penalty system that consumes substantial time and resources and hangs like a weight on our criminal courts.

Although the cost of LWOP is high, the cost of capital punishment is far higher. Studies on the cost of the death penalty versus alternative punishments date back to the 1970s. These studies have been conducted by academic researchers, public policy organizations, journalists, and commissions formed to advise legislators. Because capital punishment in the United States is mainly controlled by the states, nearly all the studies focus on individual states. Here is an overview of the findings:

- In Kansas, a report by the Judicial Council Advisory Committee concluded that cases seeking a sentence of death were 3–4 times as expensive than capital murder cases where the death penalty was not sought (Judicial Council, 2014).

- In North Carolina, data on the cost of each phase of the legal process revealed that, compared to first-degree murder cases in which the death penalty was not sought, the *extra* cost of adjudicating a capital case through to execution was $2.16 million. That figure underestimates the true cost because it includes only costs to state and local government (thus excluding all private and federal costs) (Cook & Slawson, 1993). A later study found that abolishing the death penalty in North Carolina would save about $10.8 million per year on trial costs alone (Cook, 2009).

- The cost of maintaining the death penalty in Florida was $51 million more per year than the cost of giving every person charged with capital murder a sentence of LWOP (Date, 2000).

- Focusing just on the costs of a trial, researchers in Arizona found that murder cases involving the death penalty cost more than twice as much as death penalty eligible cases where the sentence of death was not sought by prosecutors (Williams, 2001).

- Studies in Washington state found that a death penalty trial costs more than double a comparable non–death penalty trial (Larranaga & Mustard, 2004)—roughly $777,000 more per death penalty trial (Sullivan, 2015).

- In Indiana, death penalty cases costs about four times as much as murder cases in which the sentence of death was not at stake (Legislative Services Agency, 2010).

- In Oregon, death penalty cases cost from $800,000 to $1 million more than aggravated murder cases where death sentences were not sought (Kaplan et al., 2016).

- Texas kills more condemned prisoners than any other state and it is also the state that has done the most to minimize the time between trial and execution. Yet, even in Texas, each capital case costs taxpayers an average of $2.3 million, nearly three times the cost of imprisonment in a maximum-security cell for forty years (Hoppe, 1992). In Harris County, Texas, home to one of the most active execution chambers in the country, county commissioners attempted to raise taxes to cover the staggering costs of capital trials. Angry voters rejected the tax hike, so fire and ambulance services had to be cut instead. Harris County is not alone. Capital trials create a crushing

financial burden for many counties because counties bear a dispro-
portionate share of the costs.

- Even during periods when few or no executions occur, the cost of
  trials, appeals, death rows, and execution chambers can be enormous. During a twenty-three-year period, New Jersey spent more
  than $250 million on its system of capital punishment but did not
  execute a single prisoner (Forsberg, 2005). Maryland spent $186
  million over a twenty-year period to execute five people (Roman et
  al., 2008). Over a thirty-eight-year period, Pennsylvania spent $816
  million on its capital punishment system and executed only three
  people—all of whom had abandoned the costly appeals process
  (Brambila, 2016).
- In California, the most populous state—and the state which once
  had the most populous death row—the California Commission on
  the Fair Administration of Justice (CCFAJ) reported that having a
  system of capital punishment cost $137.7 million annually. In com-
  parison, a system that had LWOP as the most severe punishment
  would have cost just $11.5 million (CCFAJ, 2008).
- Finally, an analysis of thirty-two states showed that, on average, death
  penalty cases cost $1,044,326 more than comparable murder cases
  where the death penalty is not sought (McFarland, 2016).

These studies cover many states, several time periods, and use varied data
collection methods. Despite these differences, the conclusions are always
the same: Having the death penalty as an available punishment is far more
expensive than a system that has LWOP as the most severe punishment.
These costs are incredibly high and appear to be rising (Collins & Kaplan,
2019; Collins, et al., 2019).

Of course, we spend time as well as money. As soon as a defendant is
charged with a capital crime, more people must spend more time to arrive
at a final sentence. When a death sentence is at stake, every phase of the legal
process becomes more complex, more expansive, and more expensive. More
attorneys are involved, more witnesses are called, and more experts testify.
There are far more pretrial motions, and pretrial investigation and preparation take much longer. So does jury selection. The capital trial alone takes
about three times as much time as comparable murder trials where the death
penalty is not at stake. Once the trial is completed, personnel from state attorney generals' offices spend considerable time responding to appeals, state

supreme courts must spend time reviewing death sentences, and governors must spend time reviewing requests to commute death sentences.

While supporters of the death penalty may quibble with the cost estimates from a particular study, the bottom line is clear: Maintaining a system of capital punishment is far more expensive than sending murderers to prison until they die of natural causes. No credible study has reached a contrary conclusion. Even if the debilitating cost of the death penalty could be cut by half—a very unlikely event—it would still be the more expensive option. Clearly, whatever benefits Americans receive from maintaining a system of capital punishment are purchased at a very high price. The punishment of death punishes taxpayers and drains away precious resources from other parts of the criminal justice system.

Why the Death Penalty Is So Costly

One reason that maintaining the death penalty is so expensive is that capital trials are more complex and time-consuming than other criminal trials at every stage of the legal process: crime investigation, pretrial preparation, jury selection, guilt trial, penalty trial, and appeals. Most of the money is spent early in the process—on preparing for and conducting the capital murder trial.

Trial preparation begins when the district attorney's office decides to seek the death penalty. A competently conducted capital trial requires a thorough investigation of both the crime and the offender. Because of the penalty phase, defense investigators will attempt to locate and interview anyone who may be able to offer testimony that can serve as mitigating evidence (e.g., members of the defendant's family, friends, co-workers, neighbors, and teachers). The personal history of the defendant is painstakingly reconstructed in an effort to explain the defendant's crime, and such carefully conducted investigations frequently take as long as two years to complete. The use of various experts—mental health professionals, medical experts, forensic scientists, and jury selection consultants—also adds to the costs. Finally, pretrial motions (i.e., requests for rulings from the judge on various legal issues) are numerous and complex.

The process of selecting jurors also takes longer in capital trials. Few prospective jurors are able or willing to commit themselves to participating in a trial that may last weeks or maybe even months. Attorneys in capital cases are permitted to excuse more jurors than usual for no stated reason, and, because death is at stake, attorneys are given greater latitude in questioning potential jurors. Thus, jury pools must be larger. In some states, jurors are questioned individually so that their answers will not influence other potential jurors. As noted in Chapter 2, capital trials include the added complication of death qualification. Finally, attorneys take more time during *voir dire* because jurors are being selected for two trials — a guilt trial and a separate penalty trial. For these reasons, jury selection takes about five times longer in capital trials than in non–capital murder trials (Haney, 2005).

Attorneys in capital cases must investigate and prepare for a charge of first-degree murder *and* other felony charges that qualify the crimes as capital (e.g., murder in the course of rape or robbery). Because of the enormous workload, both defense and prosecution teams usually include at least two attorneys and many investigators. The need to formulate a guilt-phase strategy that complements the penalty-phase strategy further complicates the job of prosecutors and defenders. Capital guilt phases consume ten to twenty times as many attorney labor-hours as non-capital cases, and capital trials generally last three times longer than comparable non-capital trials (Foglia & Sandys, 2018). Most important, the extra costs associated with capital trials are incurred *not only* when a defendant is sentenced to death, but *also* when a defendant is acquitted or sentenced to life imprisonment. Since only a minority of capital offenders are sentenced to death, most of the money that is spent to maintain our system of capital punishment is spent on the lengthy, expensive trials of defendants who end up being sentenced to life imprisonment. Consequently, the price tag per death sentence is astronomical.

Although most of the money spent on capital punishment is spent before appeals even begin, the labyrinthine appeals process for capital cases is also expensive. Capital appeals generally cost more than non-capital appeals because of the complexity of the legal issues involved, the number of different issues that can be raised, and the availability of multiple avenues for appeal (Griffin & Griffin, 2018; Latzer & Cauthen, 2007).

Because a high proportion of death sentences are reversed on appeal (roughly 38%; Baumgartner & Dietrich, 2017), and because the defendant's life is at stake, there is ample incentive for pursuing every avenue of appeal. When an appeal is successful, the state must bear the costs of a capital trial and the costs of the appeals process, *as well* as the cost of imprisoning the convict for life. This is a crucial point for understanding the true cost of the death penalty: We pay the high price of a capital trial *not only* when a defendant is sentenced to death, but *also* when a defendant is sentenced to life imprisonment. Fewer than a third of capital trials culminate in a sentence of death, and the number of death sentences has steadily declined (from a high of 315 in 1996 to a low of just 18 in 2021). For the minority of defendants who do receive a death sentence, we pay for an expensive capital trial *and* an expensive appeals process. When an appeal is successful, the state bears the cost of defending the death sentence *in addition to* the cost of life imprisonment.

The price tag for capital punishment also includes the considerable expense of operating death rows—expensive maximum-security units within large penitentiaries. As many analysts have noted, the demands of running a death row create frustrating problems for prison officials. "Without the sentence of death, the condemned would not necessarily be the most dangerous prison inmates demanding the limited single cells available for strict security. In consequence, the prison system is severely restricted in its ability to find secure space for its own troublemakers" (Nakell, 1987, p. 245). The mere existence of death row has an unsettling effect on the entire prison population, and, during the days preceding and following a scheduled execution, disruptive behavior surges (Johnson, 2019).

Compared to the massive costs of capital trials, appeals, and incarceration on death row, the cost of building, maintaining, and operating an execution chamber is only a tiny drop in a large bucket. But it is worth mentioning. The chamber and the additional personnel time needed to maintain and operate the execution machinery and to prepare the condemned prisoner for death also adds to the cost. Like cars and computers, the execution technology must be serviced, repaired, and occasionally replaced.

Most defendants accused of capital crimes do not die in the execution chamber. Some aren't convicted, many are convicted but not sentenced to death, many have their death sentence reversed on appeal, a few have their death sentences commuted, and many die in prison before they can be marched to the execution chamber. Still, the vast and intricate procedural machinery of capital punishment must continue to be financed. Massive resources are squandered, courts and prisons are strained just so that, eventually, a few condemned prisoners can be killed. Whatever satisfaction we receive from executions must be weighed against the time and money spent to sustain our system of capital punishment.

The true price of the death penalty looms even larger when one considers what economists call "opportunity costs"—in this case, the value of what could have been purchased if the death penalty had not been purchased. Put differently, the tremendous sums of money expended each year to maintain a system of capital punishment could be spent more productively elsewhere, for example, on programs designed to prevent or reduce crime. As former police Chief put it,

> I learned that the death penalty throws millions of dollars down the drain—money that I could be putting directly to work fighting crime every day—while dragging victims' families through a long and torturous process that only exacerbates their pain. . . . Give a law enforcement professional like me that $250 million, and I'll show you how to reduce crime. The death penalty isn't anywhere on my list. (Abbot, 2009, p. 2)

Many states have been forced to take extraordinary steps to deal with shrinking budgets. Early intervention, education, and anti-poverty programs have been cut. Yet, in the states that retain it, capital punishment has been spared by budget cutters. By focusing on killing a handful of individual offenders, we divert precious attention and millions of dollars away from reforms that address the causes of violent crime.

Streamlining the System to Cut Costs

It might be possible to simplify our system of capital punishment and thereby reduce its total cost. Over the past three decades, some streamlining in the appeals process has already occurred (Griffin & Griffin, 2018). However, further streamlining is unwise and unlikely for several reasons.

In fashioning a system of capital jurisprudence that passes constitutional muster, the Supreme Court has repeatedly emphasized that the punishment of death is qualitatively different from all other punishments because of its severity and irrevocability. This "death is different" doctrine holds that capital defendants are entitled to what has been called "super due process." This includes the trial and appeals procedures discussed above. As Justice O'Connor observed,

> Among the most important and consistent themes in the Court's death penalty jurisprudence is the need for special care and deliberation in decisions that may lead to the imposition of that sanction. The Court has accordingly imposed a series of unique substantive and procedural

restrictions designed to ensure that capital punishment is not imposed without the serious and calm reflection that ought to precede any decision of such gravity and finality. (*Thompson v. Oklahoma*, 1988, p. 856)

The unique procedural safeguards alluded to by Justice O'Connor include separate guilt and penalty trials, great latitude in presenting mitigating evidence during the penalty phase of the trial, automatic appeal to the state supreme court, and a variety of opportunities for judicial review of death sentences. The current system was developed over several decades in an effort to increase fairness and prevent arbitrary or discriminatory sentences of death. There is no alternative bargain basement version of justice in death penalty cases.

Any further attempt to bypass current safeguards would likely violate the constitutional rights of the defendant, exacerbate racially discriminatory death sentencing, and increase the number of innocent people sent to the execution chamber. Even with current safeguards in place, a substantial number of capital convictions and death sentences are overturned on appeal because of errors. That is, because of errors or biases at the initial trial, appeals courts reduce death sentences to LWOP or exonerate the person on death row. For example, a large-scale study of trials that culminated in a death sentence identified 616 cases that were later reversed because of misconduct (Death Penalty Information Center [DPIC], 2022). These reversals were not because of mere legal technicalities: They were the result of fundamental errors and outright misconduct, such as the withholding of exculpatory evidence by police or prosecutors, improper arguments by prosecutors, false or fabricated evidence, racial discrimination in jury selection, and inadequate assistance of defense counsel. Indeed, one massive study of every capital case in the United States over a twenty-two-year time span found that 68% of death sentences were reversed because of serious errors at trial (Liebman et al., 2000).

It is not entirely clear why there is a such a high rate of reversals in death penalty cases. Perhaps public outrage and media attention create pressure for a speedy conviction and pressure to seek the death penalty. Court-appointed attorneys and some public defenders are overworked and often inexperienced in capital cases. Prosecutors may pursue the death penalty in questionable cases as a means of advancing their own careers. Judges who later review the cases may simply be more willing to reverse a sentence of death because a death sentence is uniquely severe.

The enhanced procedural protections afforded the capital defendant are designed to eliminate error—to ensure that only those guilty of the most egregious crimes are sentenced to death. If errors had in fact been eliminated, then perhaps the entire system might be streamlined without increasing the risk of error. Unfortunately, the available data reveal that even our current elaborate system permits significant errors. The most troubling form of error in capital cases is the conviction, imprisonment, or execution of an innocent person. Of course, our criminal justice system is far from infallible and there is strong evidence that such extreme miscarriages of justice do occur (see Chapter 7). Even the most ardent supporters of capital punishment do not want to increase the probability of convicting or executing innocent defendants.

In sum, there is considerable evidence that Americans will save money when the death penalty is abolished. Streamlining the legal system might reduce costs, but the moral consequences of streamlining (e.g., violations of constitutional rights, increased capriciousness, a rise in wrongful convictions and executions) are unacceptably high.

Capital punishment must be defended or challenged on the basis of a cost-benefit analysis. In the absence of compelling evidence that the death penalty reduces violent crime and makes our streets safer, wise policymakers should choose the cheaper option of LWOP and spend the savings on crime prevention. This would ease the strain on the legal system, prevent the execution of innocents, and free up the substantial time and resources that are poured into our current system of capital punishment.

7

Are There Errors and Biases in the Application of the Death Penalty?

NO ONE BELIEVES OUR CRIMINAL justice system is infallible. One common criticism is that judges and juries are too soft and that sometimes real criminals go free or serve short sentences. Clearly there is truth in this claim. Still, we must not close our eyes to the reality of error in the opposite direction, the reality that sometimes the system wrongfully arrests, convicts, imprisons, and occasionally even executes an innocent person. This is the most troubling form of error in capital cases. No reasonable person genuinely believes that our system is so perfectly constructed and calibrated that such mistakes never happen. However, since some reasonable people do seem to believe that such errors are a thing of the past, here are a few recent examples:

- Sherwood Brown was released from death row in Mississippi in 2021. He had been sentenced to death for the murder of a thirteen-year-old girl, her mother, and her grandmother. At his trial, a jailhouse informant falsely claimed that Brown had confessed to the killings while in jail, two forensic odontologists (dentists who analyze bitemarks to identify the biter) testified that a bruise on Brown's wrist was actually a bitemark that matched the tooth pattern of the murdered girl, and the prosecution argued that a trace of blood found on one of Brown's shoes came from one of the victims. In the years following the conviction, more careful analysis of the physical evidence revealed that Brown's DNA was not in the saliva of the victim, that the blood on the sole of his shoe was from a male, and that the autopsy of the victim found DNA from two unidentified males on the victim's body, but no DNA from Brown. Also, fingerprints and hair at the scene did not match Brown.

- In 2022, prosecutors moved to dismiss all charges against Marilyn Mulero. She had been sentenced to death in 1993. Mulero was twenty-one when she and fifteen-year-old Jacqueline Montanez were charged with luring two men from the Latin Kings gang to a park in Chicago, where both men were shot and killed. The prosecution argued at trial that the victims were murdered in retaliation for an earlier killing by a rival gang. Mulero had friends who were members of that gang. She was interrogated for more than twenty hours and intimidated by a notoriously corrupt detective who threatened her with a death sentence and having her children taken from her. That detective (Reynaldo Guevara) was later implicated in framing more than forty innocent people. Mulero eventually signed a confession written by the detectives. In addition to the "confession," there was an eyewitness (later revealed to be the girlfriend of one of victims) who claimed to have seen Mulero shoot one of the men. The eyewitness claimed to have seen the shooting after midnight, from her apartment window, more than four-hundred feet away (Brooks, 2023). In 2017, Montanez admitted that she had committed both murders and that Mulero had become frightened and ran away (the story that Mulero had told from the beginning).

- Walter Barton was executed by the state of Missouri in 2020 for the vicious murder of an eighty-one-year-old woman who had been stabbed more than thirty times. He had been tried five times: The first trial ended in a mistrial and the second ended with a hung jury. Barton's conviction in the third trial was overturned because the trial judge unfairly restricted the defense arguments. Barton was convicted again in his fourth trial. But that conviction was overturned because of prosecutorial misconduct. The fifth trial ended in a conviction and sentence of death.

  A key piece of testimony against Barton came from a jailhouse informant who claimed that Barton had confessed to her that he had committed the murder. The informant further claimed that Barton said he would kill her "like he killed that old lady" if she told anyone. Prosecutors failed to disclose that they had dismissed one of the cases against the informant in exchange for her testimony. There was also questionable blood spatter evidence. Barton, a neighbor of the victim, and the victim's granddaughter discovered the victim's dead, blood-soaked body. Barton maintained that he had pulled the granddaughter from her grandmother's bloody dead body, getting some of the victim's blood on his clothes. The granddaughter corroborated this claim. However, at trial, an expert witness and the prosecutor portrayed those droplets of blood as "impact stains" resulting from "high velocity" blood spatter that could only have occurred during the act of stabbing. A later analysis, however, concluded that the stains on Barton's clothes were likely "transfer stains" caused by contact with other bloodstains. That later analysis also concluded that the actual murderer would have been covered in blood. Prior to his execution, three jurors who had voted to convict Barton signed affidavits saying that the newer bloodstain analysis would have changed their votes during their guilt-stage deliberations at trial.

- John Huffington was exonerated in 2023. He had been convicted and sentenced to death for two murders. One victim, Diane Becker, was found beaten to death in her RV, and her boyfriend, Joseph Hudson, was found a few miles away fatally shot. A second suspect in the slayings, Deno Kanaras, testified against Huffington. Kanaras told police he was present when Huffington committed the murders during a drug deal and robbery. Huffington maintained his innocence and claimed that he was not at either crime scene.

  FBI agents analyzed physical trace evidence from the crime scenes. One agent testified that hairs recovered from Becker's bed and clothing, "microscopically matched the head hairs of Mr. Huffington—that is, they are indistinguishable from Mr. Huffington's head hairs; you could not tell them apart." Another agent testified that the bullets extracted from Hudson's body could have been fired by a revolver recovered in a pool of water near the scene of the shooting and that shell casings found near his body were fired from that same gun "to the exclusion of all other revolvers" (National Registry of Exonerations [NRE], 2023). Finally, there was testimony that the bullets had the same chemical composition as bullets that had been recovered from Hudson's body and that a fingerprint on the vodka bottle in the RV was made by Huffington's right index finger. Not only was the evidence presented at trial scientifically invalid, but the prosecutor also withheld and misrepresented other evidence that exculpated Huffington.

The long and growing list of people wrongfully convicted of capital murder stands at 199 since 1973, and the number of people who were executed but probably innocent stands at 20 (Death Penalty Information Center [DPIC], 2024). Descriptions of their cases could easily fill the remainder of this book. But it is essential to look beneath the numbers to expose the underlying causes of these fatal errors. Every such error creates two terrible tragedies. The first tragedy is the unimaginable suffering of the person who is wrongfully convicted. Most spend years on death row, some spend decades on death row, and some are even killed in the execution chamber. The second tragedy is that the actual murderer remains free. Many who escape conviction continue to commit horrible crimes before the legal system finally catches up with them, if it catches up with them at all. Of course, these additional crimes create great suffering for additional victims.

It is likely that the number of proven errors vastly underestimates the incidence of "wrong person" errors. It is impossible to know how many erroneous convictions are never discovered or remedied. Although a condemned prisoner may claim to be innocent, he is in no position to prove it. Proving innocence and getting the courts to listen to new evidence are almost always the result of the tireless efforts of defense lawyers, family members, or journalists. These efforts must yield results *before* the prisoner is led to the execution chamber. The incentive for further investigation goes to the grave with the executed prisoner, and the case is usually closed with the coffin. Once the inmate has been killed, defense attorneys, investigators, and journalists turn their attention to other cases, cases where the defendant is still alive. Better to spend limited time and money on those defendants who still might be rescued before their date with the executioner. Add to these problems the deep reluctance of officials to admit serious error, and it becomes clear why the conviction and execution of innocent people is severely underestimated.

Most of the typical causes of wrongful convictions in capital cases are visible in the four cases described above. Here is a list of the leading causes: misconduct by police or prosecutors (e.g., sloppy or corrupt investigations or failing to disclose exculpating evidence to defense lawyers or misrepresenting evidence at trial), false accusation (often by the actual perpetrator or someone connected to him), perjury (e.g., by a jailhouse snitch who claims the defendant confessed to him while in jail awaiting trial), unreliable or invalid forensic identification evidence (e.g., bite mark analysis, bullet composition analysis, microscopic hair comparisons, blood spatter patterns), inadequate defense lawyers who fail to mount a competent defense (e.g., by not fighting to exclude unreliable evidence, by not calling essential witnesses, or by failing to effectively cross-examine prosecution witnesses), a false confession (extracted from a vulnerable suspect through coercive interrogation tactics or by police lying about evidence), or a mistaken eyewitness who falsely identifies the defendant (Innocence Project, 2023a). Many wrongful convictions have more than one of these contributing factors.

One of the clearest ways to establish innocence is through DNA evidence. Indeed, many death row exonerees have been released because of DNA evidence—for example, if the victim was raped and murdered, DNA from semen left at the crime scene might not belong to the man on death row. However, even though DNA is the strongest form of forensic identification evidence, it is not always available or definitive. DNA might not have been left behind (e.g., someone may have been shot from a distance and the gun may not have been recovered), DNA might not have been collected at the crime scene, DNA may have been collected but not preserved for later testing, or it may have been stored in a way that allowed the sample to decay. And, in some cases, the defendant's DNA may have been found on the victim but was likely there before the murder (e.g., when a man returns home to find his wife has been killed). For these reasons, only about 15% of innocent death row inmates have been released because of DNA evidence (Harmon & Falco, 2018). The list of death row exonerees also include those who have been acquitted of all charges, those for whom the prosecution has dismissed all charges, and those who have been granted a pardon because of evidence of innocence.

Once a defendant has been convicted and sentenced to death it is very difficult to overturn that conviction on appeal unless persuasive new evidence of innocence has been uncovered. For example, to overturn a conviction based on ineffective assistance of counsel, that lawyer must have "performed below an objective standard of reasonableness," and there must be "a reasonable probability that, if the lawyer had performed adequately, the result would have been different" (Brooks, 2023). This vague, subjective standard allows judges to conclude that even egregiously ineffective representation was essentially "harmless" and would not have altered the verdict.

The factor most responsible for the discovery of new evidence of innocence is almost always the hiring or appointment of a new lawyer who was not involved in the initial trial. Researchers who have analyzed wrongful capital conviction cases reached the following conclusion:

> The discovery of errors and new evidence that resulted in exoneration are usually the result of hard work and dogged investigation by defense attorneys whose dedication goes above and beyond the normal standards and requirements of appellate attorneys. . . . In many exoneration capital cases, the attorneys worked pro bono for many years before seeing their clients exonerated. . . . In many, if not most cases, the system had nothing to do with the new evidence coming to light. (Harmon & Falco, 2018, p. 580)

There is, of course, no guarantee that a death row inmate will get a lawyer who will go "above and beyond the normal standards and requirements." Most lawyers do not. Unfortunately, without the help of a skilled, dedicated lawyer, the innocent inmate is likely to languish on death row. For a lucky few, there is another narrow road out: A small but significant number of people on death row have been exonerated largely because of the involvement of an outside group—the Innocence Project, a team of journalists, documentary film makers, or podcasters. Since the reinstatement of the death penalty in 1977, a total of 194 people sentenced to death have been exonerated (DPIC, 2024). A study of people sentenced to death found that 4% were actually innocent. The average time these innocent people spent on death row was eleven years, and the longest time served was thirty-nine years (Gross et al., 2014).

The fortunate few who are eventually exonerated face special problems and challenges. There is the shock and terror of being convicted and sentenced to death for a crime they did not commit. There are the standard deprivations, traumas, and pains of learning to survive in prison; plus the long-term psychological effects of near solitary confinement on death row; plus the fear of being executed before they can prove their innocence. There are the emotional ups and downs of legal battles. While incarcerated, they frequently must grieve the deaths of loved ones, endure divorces, and live with the sadness of knowing that their children are growing up without them. Once exonerated and released, they must learn how to navigate their new lives in a dramatically altered world. Finally, there is the enduring stigma of having been convicted of a capital crime. Despite their exoneration and release from prison, some people still refuse to acknowledge their innocence. Researchers who interviewed many exonerees described the reception received by one of them: "He was greeted with fear from his neighbors, suspicion from people he had known since childhood, and messages of hate written in the dirt on his truck—'child killer'" (Westervelt & Cook, 2012, p. 166).

Beyond the well-documented evidence that mistakes continue to accumulate, there is no rational basis for believing that innocent people have become substantially better protected against wrongful executions because of reforms in our legal system. For nearly a century, researchers and legal scholars have suggested a series of reforms that would help to reduce (but not eliminate) "wrong person" errors (Borchard, 1932; Frank & Frank, 1957; Holloway, 2021; Innocence Project, 2023b; Kruse, 2015). However, there has been only modest progress in adopting these well-considered but often expensive and time-consuming reforms. As discussed earlier, the only major procedural reforms in capital cases were the result of the *Gregg v. Georgia* decision of 1976. These reforms, which included introduction of the two-phase trial and automatic appeals in capital cases, did not directly address what we now know to be the major sources of error in capital cases: suppressed or fabricated evidence, mistaken eyewitness identification, shoddy investigation, corrupt prosecutors, or incompetent defense lawyering.

The Geography of Death

Death sentences and executions are strongly influenced by geography. The most obvious geographic variation is that many states have the death penalty, and many do not. Looking across states that retain the death penalty, we find significant interstate variation in the instructions given to the jurors who must make the life-or-death decision (see Chapter 2) and in how prosecutors in different states (and across counties within each state) use their discretion when deciding whether to seek the death penalty in individual cases. And, when we look at the number of executions by state, the disparities are glaring. Between 2020 and 2023, most states with the death penalty executed no one. Eighty-five percent of executions during that period were carried out in just five states: Texas, Oklahoma, Missouri, Alabama, and Florida. A full third of all executions in that period were carried out in Texas alone. The death penalty in America has become increasingly confined to the southern states. Missouri—a state that borders the American South—is the only exception.

There are also significant disparities *within* each death penalty state. When researchers looked at sentencing patterns by county, they found that death sentences are highly clustered. An analysis of death penalty states over a six-year period found that 90% of all counties did not sentence anyone to death. Among the 10% of counties that did sentence one or more person to death, only 4% of those counties sentenced two or more people to death. These counties were responsible for 76% of all death sentences handed down over the six-year period analyzed (Smith, 2012).

Researchers have also found huge cross-county variations in prosecutor's decisions to charge capital murder in eligible cases. An early study of South Carolina's sixteen judicial districts found that rates of charging an eligible case as capital murder ranged from a low of 16.7% in one district to a high of 86.7% in another (Paternoster, 1991). In a more recent study, the county with the lowest rate filed charges for capital murder in 1.9% of eligible cases, and the county with the highest rate charged capital murder in 14.9% of cases (Songer & Unah, 2006). Put differently, the same state standards for seeking the death penalty were applied very differently across counties within that state. Similarly, if we look within two of the states that hand down the most death sentences—Texas and Florida—we find that death sentences are concentrated in a handful of counties. Texas has 254 counties, but only 4 (Harris, Bexar, Tarrant, and Dallas) returned more than one death sentence per year. Florida has 67 counties, but only 3 (Doval, Broward, and Polk) averaged more than two death sentences a year. These counties are not those with the highest populations or the highest murder rates. Indeed, most are suburban counties with smaller populations and lower murder rates than urban counties (Trahan et al., 2018).

All the Justice Money Can Buy

Few Americans doubt that the legal system treats rich people better than poor people. Although in principle every defendant has access to the same constitutional rights, in practice, full use of those rights costs money—lots of it. And the people who end up on trial for capital murder tend to be poor. As Justice William O. Douglas observed, "One searches our chronicles in vain for the execution of any member of the affluent strata of this society." Some residents of death row put it even more succinctly: "It's called capital punishment because if you don't have the capital, you get the punishment."

Nearly thirty years ago, in what was called "the trial of the century," a rich man went on trial for a vicious double murder. Orenthal James Simpson (aka, O. J.) was tried for the savage murder of his former wife, Nicole Brown Simpson, and her friend Ronald Goldman. Mr. Simpson was handsome and charming, a record-setting football hero, a persuasive pitchman for several products, and a sometime movie actor. Most important, he was a multimillionaire.

One of the first decisions faced by prosecutors was whether to seek the death penalty. They decided not to. That decision might have been reasonable. Because O. J. was a celebrity, it might have been difficult to persuade a jury to sentence him to death. Political pressures may also have been at play—the DA had been elected with strong support from the Black community, and leaders in that community made it clear that they would prefer that the death penalty not be at stake. But, as many critics of that decision pointed out at the time, prosecutors had good reasons to seek the death penalty—there were, after all, two victims, and both of their throats had been brutally slashed, leaving them nearly decapitated. There was also a history of violence: Simpson had been arrested as a teenager, he had pleaded no contest to a charge of spousal abuse five years earlier, and there was clear evidence of recurrent spouse battering. The history of violence, the vicious nature of the crime, and the number of victims might have been used to justify a decision to seek the death penalty. The crucial point is that wealth and status tipped the scales of justice in Mr. Simpson's favor from the earliest stages in the process.

A decision not to seek a death sentence changes the dynamics of the case (see Chapter 2). Jurors in capital cases must be "death qualified": Prospective jurors who claim that they are incapable of voting for death are automatically excused from service. Because death-qualified jurors tend to be more conviction prone than those not death-qualified, the probability of an acquittal is increased when prosecutors decide not to seek the death penalty (Haney et al., 2022). Subsequent decisions were also influenced by Mr. Simpson's wealth. His preliminary hearing lasted much longer than most, with defense attorneys vigorously asserting the rights of their client. Within four months, the trial had commenced. Eleven defense lawyers appeared in court on behalf of O. J., and more worked behind the scenes. The full defense team also included private investigators, jury selection consultants, and several highly paid expert witnesses who challenged every claim made by the prosecution and presented alternative interpretations of the evidence. Huge amounts of time and money were poured into the trial—it lasted more than eight months and produced more than 45,000 pages of testimony. At the time, the total cost for the defense was estimated to be somewhere between $6 million and $8 million. The final verdict was "not guilty."

When one of Simpson's lawyers was asked whether O. J. bought a not-guilty verdict, the lawyer responded, "O. J. didn't buy justice; every defendant deserves the kind of defense O. J. was able to afford." In one sense, he was clearly right. If you or someone you loved was accused of murder, you would surely want a defense team as skillful and thorough as O. J.'s. Of course, the critical point is that only a miniscule number of people charged with murder can afford the kind of defense he was able to buy.

In contrast, consider the case of Ernest Dwayne Jones. His trial took place down the hall from Simpson's. Mr. Jones stood accused of raping and viciously stabbing his girlfriend's mother until she died. Her body was found with two kitchen knives sticking out of her neck. There were no eyewitnesses. Jones suffered from psychological disorders, had a history of being sexually abused, and had grown up with two alcoholic parents. He also had a previous history of violence. Ten years prior, he had been convicted of rape, and he had served six years in prison. Jones only had one lawyer; a public defender appointed by the state. The prosecution's DNA evidence, which was analyzed by the same company used in the Simpson case, was presented in a day. Unlike in the Simpson trial, there were no renowned defense experts to raise suspicions about contamination of the DNA sample or bias in the laboratory analysis. There was no additional defense attorney with special expertise in DNA evidence to grill the prosecution expert. In fact, in the Jones trial, the DNA expert was not even cross-examined by the defender. The entire trial lasted twelve days and Jones was found guilty. It took another three days to complete the penalty phase and sentence Mr. Jones to death. When asked to compare the two trials, the foreman of the Jones jury said, "If they brought in other experts and overwhelmed us with clever data and impressive people, they might at least have got the jury to hang . . . and if he [Jones] had gotten [Simpson's] lawyers and his resources, he [Jones] wouldn't be sentenced to death" (Feldman, 1995). But Jones, like the vast majority of capital defendants, couldn't afford the team of lawyers and experts that might have averted a sentence of death.

Imagine that you have been charged with capital murder. Perhaps it was a case of mistaken identity, perhaps you had to kill in self-defense, maybe someone you were with pulled the trigger. You would want a swift, thorough investigation of the crime; you would want all potential witnesses interviewed; you would want experts to sift painstakingly through the physical evidence; you would want to hire a jury selection expert; and you would want to hire your own experts to contradict the prosecution's experts. Most of all, you would want the best, most experienced defense attorneys you could find. The lawyers are crucial. They prepare the case, locate and prepare the witnesses, file motions, cross-examine prosecution witnesses, help explain slippery concepts (like premeditation, aggravation, and mitigation) to the jury, object to improper questions by the prosecution, and fight to get favorable evidence admitted and unfavorable evidence excluded. All these services are available to every American—for a price. If the price is more than you can afford, you are entitled to a court-appointed attorney, but not necessarily a good or experienced attorney. Although in many jurisdictions there are excellent public defenders with experience in trying capital cases, there are still many locations that rely on poorly paid, inexperienced private attorneys. Maybe you'll get lucky and wind up with a team of capable defense attorneys. But would you be willing to bet your life on it?

The sad, shameful fact is that money makes the difference between life and death for many defendants. Far too often, it is not those who commit the most despicable crimes who are sent to death row, but those who lack the money to mount an adequate defense. Money can buy a thorough investigation of the crime, expert analysis of evidence, expert testimony, and a careful search for mitigating factors that may need to be presented during a penalty phase. Most important, money can buy skilled, experienced lawyers. Rich people can afford to select their lawyers, but poor people are at the mercy of the attorney assigned to them.

Because few capital defendants can afford to hire their own lawyer, they are represented by either a public defender or a court-appointed private attorney. Public defenders work for state-funded offices that specialize in representing indigent clients. Fortunately, there are many dedicated public defenders who are both capable and experienced in defending people accused of capital crimes, and these defenders manage to provide effective representation despite low pay and heavy workloads. But there are not nearly enough to go around. Most public defenders' offices are located in large cities, and many counties in many states have no such office. In these states, capital defendants are represented by court-appointed lawyers: private attorneys assigned by trial judges.

The effectiveness of defense attorneys in capital cases varies wildly. Many states have a cap on spending for each capital trial. Stephen Bright, a lawyer who has defended many capital defendants, reports that his pay for representing some capital defendants in the South amounted to less than minimum wage. He notes that in many capital cases, the court reporter is paid more than the lawyer appointed to defend the accused (Bright & Kwak, 2023). Because of unrealistic limits on the total amount of money the state allocates for the defense of a capital client, the available funds are often exhausted before the trial even begins.

Moreover, in most cases, the balance of resources between defense and prosecution is not equal. Like public defenders, prosecutors tend to carry a heavy caseload. But they tend to be better paid, and they have considerably more resources at their disposal. Typically, defenders must file motions to fund investigations, obtain laboratory analysis of physical evidence, and hire psychologists or jury experts or expert witnesses. In contrast, prosecutors are able to use the local police forces as their investigators, and they have access to crime labs and pathologists from the coroner's office. While court-appointed lawyers are often inexperienced and not fully conversant with the relevant law, prosecutors' offices are staffed with experienced attorneys, and even novice prosecutors have ready access to the expertise of more seasoned colleagues. Outside of public defenders' offices, there is no comparable network for defense attorneys in capital trials.

There are dozens of stories of dangerously deficient defense lawyering in capital cases. Some attorneys have slept through parts of their client's trial, some were drunk or under the influence of drugs during trial, some simply failed to prepare for trial, and some provided only a perfunctory defense (e.g., failing to effectively cross-examine prosecution witnesses, failing to object when warranted, failing to find qualified experts to testify). Closing arguments to the jury in the penalty phase can also be woefully inadequate. Here is the entire penalty-phase closing argument of one court-appointed lawyer: "You are an extremely intelligent jury. You've got that man's life in your hands. You can take it or not. That's all I have to say" (Hanson, 1995). Hardly the impassioned, eloquent appeal we would hope for when a defendant's life is at stake. Unsurprisingly, the defendant was sentenced to death.

As Justice Thurgood Marshall observed, many court-appointed private attorneys,

> are handling their first criminal cases, or their first murder cases, when confronted with the prospect of a death penalty. Though acting in good faith, they inevitably make very serious mistakes. . . . The federal courts are filled with stories of counsel who presented no evidence in mitigation of their client's sentence because they did not know what to offer or how to offer it or had not read the state's sentencing statute. (*Woodson v. North Carolina*, 1976)

Advocates of the death penalty might argue that most errors resulting from deficient lawyering are remedied on appeal. But a sloppy, cursory defense at trial has lasting effects on the defendant's prospects on appeal. Clearly, the appeals process can correct some errors. But the process is far from perfect. There are significant legal barriers to making an appeal based on issues that were not raised in the initial trial. To preserve a claim for later appeal, an attorney must often raise the relevant issue (e.g., admission of improper incriminating evidence or failure to admit crucial exculpating evidence) during the initial trial. Otherwise, the defendant may forfeit the right to have the claim considered on appeal. Furthermore, the defendant must show that the lawyer's mistakes were serious enough to violate the constitutional right to "effective assistance of counsel." Recent Supreme Court decisions make it necessary for appellate lawyers to prove that the errors were consequential enough to change the outcome of the case (Primus, 2020).

There is considerable discretion at every choice point in our system of capital punishment—to arrest or not, to charge or not, to plea bargain or to go to trial, to seek the death penalty or not, to convict or acquit, to sentence to life in prison or death by execution, and on what grounds to appeal a conviction or sentence. Securing the effective assistance of skilled, experienced lawyers is essential. If you are rich, finding such lawyers is easy. If you are poor, you need to be lucky. The constitutional scholar, Charles Black Jr. made the point forcefully.

Can you really doubt that a process like this, from first to last, is heavily loaded against the poor? Could you really be surprised at the finding that by far the majority of people suffering death are poor? Are you satisfied with that? If you are not, face the fact that there is no way to change it except to do away with the death penalty. (Black, 1974, p. 91)

Justice in Black and White

During the time of slavery there was no pretense of equal justice. Slaves were regarded as property and slave owners could abuse their property in nearly any way they saw fit. The so-called Black Codes stipulated in law that Black people could be treated far more severely than White people for similar crimes. Prior to the Civil War in the South, Black people could be put to death for a variety of crimes. The rape of a Black woman was not considered a crime, but many Black men were killed for the alleged rape of a White woman. Black people could be executed for property crimes such as burglary or arson, while White people were permitted to pay a fine or serve a short jail term. Black people faced not only harsher punishments but also formidable procedural obstacles: They could not testify in court against White people, and they could not serve on juries.

Unofficial "justice" could be even harsher than that dispensed by the official courts. Recorded lynchings numbered 1,540 during the 1890s, and another 1,951 lynchings took place between 1900 and the end of the 1930s. The yearly number of lynchings often exceeded the number of official executions, and Black men were overwhelmingly the targets of these spontaneous killings (Vandiver, 2018). At the turn of the century, one commentator summarized the prevailing view of such punishments.

The frequent atrocity of the crimes committed by negroes of low character, without apparently any particular provocation, is something scarcely to be understood—the adjectives wanton, bestial, outrageous, brutal and inhuman all seem wholly inadequate to express the feeling of utter disgust and abhorrence that is aroused. . . . Southern Whites have found the law and its administration utterly unsuited to the function of dealing with negro criminals—hence, the frequent adoption of summary and extra-legal methods of punishment. (Cutler, 1907, p. 622)

Lynchings of Black men for the alleged rape of White women were so frequent that in newspaper accounts of the time it was simply reported that "a negro man was hanged for the usual crime." Even in more modern times, Black men have been disproportionately sentenced to death for the crime of rape. An especially thorough investigation by Marvin Wolfgang and Marc Riedel examined 361 rape convictions during the period 1945–1965 (Wolfgang & Riedel, 1973). After controlling for a variety of variables, they found that the best predictor of a death sentence was the race of the offender combined with the race of the victim. Black men convicted of raping White women were the group most likely to be sentenced to death by a shocking margin. Four hundred and fifty-five men were executed for rape between 1930 and 1967, and 89% of those men were Black. In *Coker v. Georgia* (1972), the Supreme Court ended the death penalty for rape in cases where the victim was not killed.

But that was all a long time ago. Now both Black and White individuals are subject to the same laws, and members of both groups are routinely sentenced to death for capital murders. Yet there is still a disturbing imbalance. Here are some statistics: At present, the US population is about 13.6% Black but the population of death row is 41.1% Black; since the resumption of executions in 1977, 34.3% of the people killed in the execution chamber have been Black, and 85.7% percent of the people executed were convicted of killing White individuals, even though roughly half of all murder victims in the United States are Black. Since the reinstatement of the death penalty only 33 White persons have been executed for killing a Black person, but 318 Black persons have been executed for killing a White person (Blevins & Minor, 2018; DPIC, 2023b). Perhaps such statistics are misleading or inconclusive, but even the most ardent supporters of capital punishment would concede that these striking disparities should make us suspicious.

Unfortunately, the evidence suggests that, despite four decades of legal and procedural tinkering, the death penalty remains capricious, flawed, and discriminatory. Just prior to his retirement in 1994, Justice Harry Blackmun, who had formerly supported capital punishment, concluded that "race continues to play a major role in determining who shall live and who shall die." He went on to offer an even broader repudiation.

For more than 20 years I have endeavored—indeed, I have struggled—along with a majority of this Court, to develop procedural and substantive rules that would lend more than the mere appearance of fairness to the death penalty endeavor. Rather than continue to coddle the Court's delusion that the desired level of fairness has been achieved and the need

> for regulation eviscerated, I feel morally and intellectually obligated simply to concede that the death penalty experiment has failed. . . . The problem is that the inevitability of factual, legal, and moral error gives us a system that we know must wrongly kill some defendants, a system that fails to deliver the fair, consistent, and reliable sentences of death required by the Constitution. (*Callins v. Collins*, 1994, p. 1152)

Racial bias seeps into the decision-making process at every juncture. Although the race of the defendant does influence decisions, it is primarily the race of the victim that matters. Several reviews of decades of research on race and the death penalty have concluded that there is a strong race-of-victim effect and a smaller but significant race-of-defendant effect (e.g., Baldus et al., 2012; Beckett & Evans, 2016; Blevins & Minor, 2018; Goldfarb, 2016; Bowers et al., 1984)

William Bowers and Glenn Pierce looked at 700 homicides and found that offenders whose victims were White were more than twice as likely to be indicted for first-degree murder than offenders whose victims were Black. In an examination of more than 600 murders, Michael Radelet (1989) found that while overall 70% of homicides led to first-degree murder indictments, more than 92% of Black offender–White victim murders led to first-degree indictments.

A similar pattern emerges when we examine the decision of whether to seek the death penalty. Research indicates that if the victim is White, prosecutors are more than twice as likely to seek a death sentence than if the victim is Black, and Black defendants who kill White victims are almost four times as likely to be charged with capital murder than are Black defendants who kill Black victims (Paternoster & Kazyaka, 1988). A study that looked at more than 700 murders in New Jersey during the 1980s found that the decision to seek a death sentence was strongly influenced by race of the victim. Prosecutors decided to seek a death sentence for 43% of the White victim murders but only for 28% of the Black victim murders. When researchers looked at the race of both victim and offender in combination, they found that prosecutors sought the death penalty in just over half of the Black killer–White victim cases, but in only 20% of the White killer–Black victim cases (Bienen et al., 1988). In Tennessee, prosecutors were 1.5 times more likely to seek a death sentence when the victim was White. When Black defendants were charged with murdering a White victim, prosecutors sought the death penalty 29% of the time, but if the victim was Black, they sought the death penalty only 18% of the time (DPIC, 2023). In an especially sophisticated analysis of this issue, David Baldus, George Woodworth, and Charles Pulaski (1990) found that, even after taking more than twenty relevant variables into account, prosecutors decided to seek the death penalty five times more often against killers of White people than against killers of Black people. In Colorado, seeking the death penalty was found to be 4.2 times higher for killers of White people than for killers of Black people (Radelet, 2017).

Only about a quarter of defendants convicted of capital murder are sentenced to death (there is tremendous variability from state to state). It is not entirely clear why the other three-quarters are spared. An optimistic inference might be that juries and judges are properly weighing legally relevant criteria and sending only the worst, most barbarous criminals to the execution chamber. There is some evidence to support this inference. Several studies have found that the probability of a death sentence is increased when there is more than one victim, when there is another violent felony (e.g., rape), if the victim was a child or elderly, and when the murder was especially brutal (Lyman et al., 2022; Paternoster, 1991). Clearly, these are factors that are legitimate to consider when making the life-or-death decision. But these are not the only factors that are considered.

Decisions about whether to seek the death penalty occur before the trial begins. It would be comforting to think that any biases that infect early decisions are somehow corrected during the later stages—that is, during the guilt and penalty phases. Unfortunately, the research shows that later stages only amplify the bias. In a large-scale study of capital sentencing in four states, William Bowers and Glenn Pierce (1980) compared the sentences of Black defendants who killed White people with the sentences of Black defendants who killed Black people in Ohio, Florida, Georgia, and Texas. In Ohio, those in the Black offender–White victim group were fifteen times more likely to receive a death sentence, in Florida they were thirty-seven times more likely, in Georgia they were thirty-three times more likely, and in Texas they were eighty-seven times more likely (Bowers & Pierce, 1980). Data from other states led to similar conclusions. For example, even after taking the characteristics of the crime into account, Gross and Mauro found that killing a White person increased the odds of being sentenced to death by a factor of four in Illinois, a factor of seven in Georgia, and a factor of nearly five in Florida (Gross & Mauro, 1989). In

Louisiana, killers of White people were more than six times more likely to receive a sentence of death than killers of Black people, and 14 times more likely to be executed (Baumgartner & Lyman, 2016).

An interesting related finding is that racial bias vanishes when the murder is especially brutal and the defendant has a history of violent crimes. When judging the worst murders, race (of the defendant or of the victim) doesn't seem to matter (Baldus et al., 1990). However, racial bias creeps in when aggravation is relatively weak and the choice between life and death is difficult. While some murders are so vicious and violent that race doesn't matter, in less brutal murders both prosecutors and jurors may unintentionally let race influence their decision-making processes. For example, although seldom discussed openly, part of the calculation in deciding whether to seek the death penalty has to do with what some prosecutors call "victim quality." The reasoning is that jurors are more likely to impose a sentence of death if the victim is easy to admire or identify with. It is easier to obtain a death sentence if the victim was a hardworking young mother than if the victim was a drug addict with a long arrest record. It is even possible that the decision not to seek the death penalty is simply a pragmatic calculation made by prosecutors who (correctly) believe that when aggravation is low or moderate, it will be more difficult to obtain a death sentence if the victim was Black.

Victim quality is not on any official list of aggravating factors. But jurors, perhaps unconsciously, assess the worth of the victim. Jurors may simply find it easier to identify with victims who are similar to them. Because most jurors in the United States are White, they may find it harder to empathize with Black victims. It is also possible that the murder of a White person may subjectively seem more frightening and personally threatening to jurors (Baldus & Woodworth, 2003; Levinson et al., 2014). If the killer is Black and the victim is White, it may have an especially strong impact on White jurors. In those cases where the argument for sending someone to the execution chamber is not overwhelming, similarity between jurors and the victim may come into play, and, in some cases, it may become the decisive factor.

Racial bias may be *especially* likely in capital cases because they arouse such strong emotions. A dispassionate, rational analysis is exceedingly difficult when confronted with a hideous crime. Also, the concepts that lie at the very heart of the penalty decision (i.e., aggravation and mitigation) are quite slippery. Because the decision must go beyond a mere mechanical weighing of facts, there is plenty of room for bias and prejudice to seep into the process. While racial and other forms of prejudice may exert little influence on factual determinations—understanding the angle of a stab wound or the trajectory of a bullet—the question of whether a defendant should live or die is saturated with subjectivity. The complex, value-laden issue of who deserves to die is thus susceptible to subtle and unconscious biases.

Several conclusions can be drawn from the research on racial disparities in capital cases: Those who are accused of murdering a White victim are more likely to be charged with a capital crime; those convicted of killing a White victim are more likely to receive a sentence of death; Black defendants convicted of killing a White person are the group most likely to receive the death penalty; White defendants who murder Black victims are the group least likely to receive a death sentence; and the effects of race are most pronounced in southern states like Texas, Georgia, Louisiana, and Florida (Blevins & Minor, 2018).

The Supreme Court's View of Race

In 1987, the US Supreme Court heard evidence about racial discrimination in the case of *McCleskey v. Kemp*. Warren McCleskey had been sentenced to death for killing a police officer during the robbery of a furniture store. A major basis for his appeal to the Supreme Court was the claim that his death sentence was the result of discrimination: He was Black and his victim was White. McCleskey had compelling evidence in his favor: an exceedingly thorough and statistically sophisticated set of studies on charging and sentencing in Georgia over a six-year period. The studies, which examined the effect of race on capital sentencing practices, were conducted by David Baldus, George Woodworth, and Charles Pulaski (1983, 1985).

Baldus and his colleagues analyzed 594 homicides in Georgia. They found that Black defendants convicted of killing White victims were sentenced to death in 22% of capital cases, whereas White defendants convicted of killing Black victims received a death sentence only 3% of the time. Taking into account more than 250 characteristics of the crime, the offender, and the victim, the researchers found that the odds of receiving a death sentence were 4.3 times higher for murderers of White people than for murderers of Black people. Based on these findings, attorneys for McCleskey argued that the racially discriminatory pattern of sentencing violated his constitutional right to equal protection under the law.

Most of the justices were unpersuaded by the data. In a sharply divided 5–4 decision, the high Court ruled that the striking pattern of racially discriminatory death sentencing did not show that McCleskey's constitutional right to equal protection had been violated. Writing for the majority, Justice Powell asserted that a successful challenge would need to prove intentional discrimination against a particular defendant. The defense would need to present "evidence specific to his own case that would support an inference that racial consideration played a part in his sentence." The Court further held that some lack of fairness was tolerable and inevitable because discretion is an essential component of any capital sentencing scheme.

Given the reasoning offered for rejecting the claim of discrimination in *McCleskey*, it is difficult to imagine a case of racial discrimination that the Supreme Court would find compelling. At least for now, the *McCleskey* decision makes it virtually impossible to demonstrate that our system of death sentencing is unconstitutional because it discriminates on the basis of race. Patterns of sentencing had been examined over a period of years, taking into consideration virtually every relevant case characteristic that could be measured. Perhaps a particular defendant could win a claim based on racial discrimination, but he or she would need to prove that the discrimination was intentional. That would be very difficult. Even when intentional racial bias influences the sentencing decision, it is rare for the decision-makers to confess that they willfully discriminated against a defendant.

Despite the court's disinterest in data showing ongoing patterns of racial discrimination in our system of capital punishment, such data continue to accumulate. Bias is still measurable at every stage of the process, from charging to sentencing to execution (Baumgartner et al., 2018; Jones, 2020; Petersen, 2017). Nonetheless, in the decades since the *McCleskey* decision, the Court has avoided dealing broadly with the role of race in death penalty decision-making (Steiker & Steiker, 2015). Instead, it has occasionally focused on specific instances of racial bias in particular cases. For example, it reversed a decision in a Texas case in which an expert witness testified at trial that the inmate posed an increased risk of dangerousness because he was Black (*Buck v. Davis*, 2017), and it also overturned the conviction of a Black man because prosecutors in the case had managed to strike nearly every potential Black juror in the jury pool over the course of the defendant's six trials (*Flowers v. Mississippi*, 2019).

Although most Supreme Court justices seem dismissive of the issue of bias and error in the administration of the death penalty, lawyers working on the frontlines appear to have serious reservations. The American Bar

Association (ABA)—the largest legal organization in the United States, with a membership including both defense and prosecuting attorneys—has called for a moratorium on executions until the inequities of the current system are corrected. Policies adopted by the ABA over the past thirty years have denounced our system of capital punishment and have recommended specific procedural reforms to reduce racial discrimination in sentencing, provide effective assistance of counsel to capital defendants, provide more thorough post-conviction review of capital cases, increase the transparency of execution protocols, and reduce the risk of executing innocent people (ABA, 2023).

Why Death Is Different

When confronted with evidence that the death penalty discriminates against African Americans and poor people, and that occasionally innocent people are convicted, sentenced to death, imprisoned, or executed, some retentionists reply that, although mistakes are regrettable, some degree of error must always be tolerated. No system will ever be perfect. The problem with this argument—as philosophers, jurists, and religious leaders have pointed out for decades—is that "death is different." That is, killing a prisoner is qualitatively different from any other form of punishment.

But what makes death unique? First, execution is the most severe form of punishment permitted in our system of justice (slow torture was long ago deemed unworthy of a civilized society). Not only is killing an extreme form of punishment, the preliminaries are also terrifying. Condemned prisoners wait in their cells for years, contemplating their fate. As appeals fail, their already meager hope evaporates, and the prisoner knows that someday a team of guards will escort him down the cell block, prepare him to be killed, and crank up the machinery that will end his life. Sister Helen Prejean, who has served as the spiritual advisor to several death row inmates, reports that many inmates are haunted by their impending doom.

> The six people that I've accompanied onto death row all had the same nightmare. The guards were dragging them from their cells. They cry for help and struggle. Then they wake up and realize that they are still in their cells. They realize it's just a dream. But they know that one day the guards are really going to come for them, and it won't be a dream. That's the torture. (Morris, 2021)

Second, the punishment of death is irrevocable. Once the prisoner has been killed, there is no possibility of reversing an error. An imprisoned man who is later found to be innocent can be released, but a corpse cannot be brought back to life. If a man is wrongly imprisoned, no amount of money can compensate him for the part of his life that has been lost, but at least he can try to enjoy what remains of his life. After an execution, it is simply too late. Even if the truth is discovered before his appointment with the executioner, the condemned prisoner will still have suffered the psychological torture of preparing to be killed and waiting for his own execution.

Because killing is a uniquely severe and final punishment, we must demand a higher standard of consistency and certainty. The harsher the punishment, the greater the need for certainty. If you receive a ticket because of a faulty parking meter, you have been treated unjustly. Still, your loss is not great. A small amount of error is tolerable. If you are wrongly imprisoned for ten years, your loss is immeasurably greater. If you are wrongly killed for a crime you did not commit, the loss is intolerable. As long as we kill as a form of punishment, such intolerable errors are inevitable.

If the legal system is permitted to kill people, killing is a penalty that ought to be reserved for the most egregious crimes. Wealth and race should not be part of the calculation. But money and color have always influenced decisions about who should be sent to the execution chamber. It is unrealistic to think that we can ever cleanse our death penalty system of such insidious influences. Even if we could, we would still occasionally convict, sentence, and execute innocent people.

Some say that we must reluctantly accept such errors as the unfortunate price for the unique benefits of executions. If the death penalty has extraordinary advantages as compared to its alternatives, perhaps it is reasonable to accept the discrimination, arbitrariness, and error that have always infected the application of capital punishment. But are there extraordinary advantages? When evaluating the benefits of any policy, there is always an implicit comparison: Beneficial compared to what? The alternative to the death penalty is life imprisonment without the possibility of parole. This alternative punishment not only satisfies our goal of protecting society, it also eliminates the risk of killing innocent people or threatening them with execution.

The only true and full solution to the problems of bias and error in our system of capital punishment is to abolish the death penalty.

8

Is Killing Murderers Morally Justified?

When faced with compelling evidence that the death penalty is costly, arbitrary, discriminatory, prone to error, and without deterrent value, retentionists often retreat into the murky waters of moral philosophy. They argue that capital punishment is not only morally legitimate, but also morally necessary. Although we can decide questions of fact—questions about cost, deterrence, fairness, and public opinion—by analyzing the relevant data, the question of whether the death penalty is ethically justified cannot be easily resolved by any amount of data. It is a matter of faith and argument. And that is precisely why many supporters of the death penalty would prefer to debate philosophy instead of effectiveness. If we are morally or religiously compelled to kill those who kill, further discussion of troublesome facts is irrelevant and unnecessary. Questions about how the ultimate penalty is administered and about the costs or the consequences of capital punishment may be interesting, but they are peripheral and do not have the power to refute a moral imperative.

The Bible Tells Me So

In their final appeals to jurors, prosecutors in capital murder trials are fond of quoting scripture to lend authority to their arguments. And there are many verses to choose from. In particular, the Old Testament seems to suggest killing as a response to a variety of crimes. The most popular quotation is from Deuteronomy 19:21: "Life for life, eye for eye, tooth for tooth, hand for hand, foot for foot." Moreover, the Old Testament recommends death for a broad assortment of crimes, including murder, contempt for parental authority, defiling sacred places or objects, kidnapping for ransom, sorcery, bestiality, worshiping false gods, profaning the Sabbath, adultery, incest, homosexuality, blasphemy, bearing false witness in court, harlotry, negligence that results in a death, and false prophesy.

Yet despite the apparent biblical endorsement of executions, there is much even in the Old Testament to suggest that killing may not be the appropriate penalty for murder. God did not kill Cain for the murder of Abel, and several cities of refuge were established so that wrongdoers could escape vengeance at the hands of their victims' families. The idea that "vengeance belongs to the Lord" and that we should "love our neighbor as ourselves" are major themes of the Bible. Even the often misinterpreted "eye for an eye" passage was meant to *restrain* rather than to *require* vengeance. Religious scholars point out that, taken in context, the passage does not tell us that we must exact proportional revenge, but that we may not take from others more than has been taken from us, that we must resist the urge to retaliate with ever greater violence (Cohn, 1970). Indeed, *Lex talionis*, the doctrine of limited legal retaliation, represented an advance, a movement away from unrestrained retaliation.

Though the Old Testament authorizes executions in principle, in practice "there were such extensive procedural requirements for the imposition of the death penalty that, by design, it was nearly impossible to secure a death verdict" (Tabak & Lane, 1989, p. 42). Mosaic law and, later, the Rabbinic tradition established a nearly unreachable standard of proof. In the Talmudic courts (called Sanhedrins), two witnesses judged to be competent had to testify that they saw the accused commit the crime after being forewarned that the act was illegal and punishable by death. Confessions were inadmissible. So was testimony against the defendant by family members of the victim or persons with a preexisting grievance against the defendant. If any aspect of the evidence or testimony was found to be unreliable, the defendant could not be killed. Such restrictions served to make capital punishment extremely rare under Talmudic law (Erez, 1981).

For Christians, the Old Testament must be interpreted in light of the New Testament, which goes much farther in repudiating revenge: "You have heard that it was said, 'An eye for an eye and a tooth for a tooth.' But I say to you, do not resist one who is evil. But if any one strikes you on the right cheek, turn to him the other also" (Matt. 5:38–41). The New

Testament emphasizes love, compassion, mercy, charity, and forgiveness. And, if we are to follow the example of Christ, forgiveness and compassion are especially important when dealing with criminals and outcasts. When Christ was confronted with a woman convicted of adultery (a capital crime at the time), the crowd who had assembled to stone her asked, "Teacher, this woman hath been taken in adultery, in the very act. Now the law of Moses commanded us to stone such: What then sayest thou of her?" In response, Jesus "lifted up himself and said unto them, 'He that is without sin among you, let him cast the first stone' (John 8:3–11). The same message can be found in Luke: "Judge not and you will not be judged; condemn not, and you will not be condemned; forgive, and you will be forgiven" (6:37). The entire life and teachings of Christ argue against killing as a form of punishment. Though not a theologian, Charles Dickens made the point well.

> Though every other man who wields a pen should turn himself into a commentator on the scriptures—not all their united efforts could persuade me that executions are a Christian law. . . . If any text appeared to justify the claim, I would reject that limited appeal, and rest upon the character of the Redeemer and the great scheme of his religion. (quoted in Koestler, 1957, p. 99)

Although the Bible can be read to support the death penalty, this support is subject to severe restrictions. Specifically, guilt must be certain, and execution must be necessary to serve the interests of justice (e.g., to protect others or to instill respect for moral authority). Indeed, no less an authority than Pope John Paul II observed that the necessary requirements for the death penalty are seldom, if ever, met. In "Evangelium Vitae" (The Gospel of Life) the Pope argued that "as explicitly formulated, the precept 'You shall not kill' is strongly negative: it indicates the extreme limit which can never be exceeded." John Paul II went on to note that punishment,

> ought not go to the extreme of executing the offender except in cases of absolute necessity: in other words, when it would not be possible otherwise to defend society. Today, however, as a result of steady improvements in the organization of the penalty system, such cases are very rare, if not practically nonexistent. . . . If bloodless means are sufficient to defend human lives against an aggressor and to protect public order and the

safety of persons, public authority must limit itself to such means. (Pope John Paul II, 1995, p. 101)

The Pope is not a lone voice among religious leaders. Religious organizations are nearly unanimous in their condemnation of capital punishment. More than forty such organizations (including the World Council of Churches, American Baptists, Catholics, Episcopalians, Jews, Lutherans, Mennonites, Methodists, Presbyterians, Quakers, and Unitarians) have issued statements calling for the abolition of capital punishment. A relatively recent statement from the United Methodist Church condemns the death penalty because it "denies the power of Christ to redeem, restore and transform human beings" and because it forecloses "the possibility of reconciliation with Christ that comes through repentance" (2016).

Moral Philosophy and the Functions of Punishment

When measured against the usual standards for evaluating punishment, the death penalty doesn't make much sense. Obviously, killing a prisoner eliminates the possibility of rehabilitation; a corpse cannot go on to lead a more virtuous life. The goal of incapacitation is not advanced: The condemned man is already safely behind prison walls, unable to commit further crimes in free society. The purported deterrent effect is illusory (see Chapter 3). And, since incapacitation and protection of society are just as effectively—and more cheaply—achieved through life imprisonment, killing the prisoner is simply unnecessary.

Moreover, how does the notion of killing murderers square with the cherished principle of "the sanctity of human life"? This idea is central to the world's great religions as well as the thinking of ancient Greek, Egyptian, Persian, and Babylonian moral philosophers. If life is sacred, it means that every person has the right to live simply by virtue of the fact that he or she is a living, breathing human being. This right is unearned and inalienable, in part (at least for those who are religious) because we are created "in the image of God." This basic principle certainly implies that the death penalty is morally wrong. However, three centuries ago, the philosopher John Locke offered a classic defense of the death penalty on moral grounds. He argued that although the right to life is inherent and absolute, it is possible to "forfeit" one's right to life by committing a crime that "deserves death." His arguments have provided ammunition for supporters of capital punishment ever since. Locke also argued for severe punishment on the grounds of deterrence. He believed that we should punish "to the degree and with as much severity, as will suffice to make it an ill bargain to the offender, give him cause to repent, and terrify others from doing the like" (Locke, 1690/1963).

Another influential moral argument is usually traced back to Immanuel Kant. He believed that murderers must be killed based on the principle of "equal" or "just" retribution.

> What kind and what degree of punishment does public legal justice adopt as its principle and standard? None other than the principle of equality ... any undeserved evil that you inflict on someone else among the people is one that you do to yourself. ... Only the law of retribution can determine exactly the kind and degree of punishment. (Kant, 1797/ 1965, p. 108)

This idea has an elegant and appealing simplicity. It is an elaboration of the idea of *lex talionis* and is similar to the argument that murderers must be "paid back" in kind for their crimes. The principle of equality introduced by Kant seems to provide a standard that is independent of religious or political authority. And whereas Locke linked his notion of retribution to deterrence, Kant apparently felt that such practical considerations were not important enough to discuss.

Another argument offered in defense of the idea that justice requires the killing of murderers might be called the "moral solidarity" argument. If societies are held together, in part, by a shared consensus of what constitutes immoral behavior, then those who violate the moral order must be punished to restore moral balance in society. Further, for murderers, any punishment less than death is too weak to convey the strong sense of outrage and condemnation felt by the community. Only by killing the murderer can we repair the moral integrity of the larger community. In his book *For Capital Punishment*, Walter Berns puts it like this:

> [The death penalty] serves to remind us of the majesty of the moral order that is embodied in our law and of the terrible consequences of its breach. ... The criminal law must be made awful, by which I mean awe-inspiring, or commanding "profound respect or reverential fear." It must remind us of the moral order by which alone we can live as human beings. (Berns, 1979, p. 194)

These arguments raise several questions. If, by killing, murderers forfeit their right to live, does that mean that we are, in turn, *obliged* to kill them? Or will other forms of severe punishment suffice? If someone *deserves* to die, does it mean that we have the right to kill him? Should we try to induce in prisoners the equivalent amount of suffering they induced in their victims? Do executions really strengthen the moral solidarity of the community, or do they demean and corrupt the collective morality? Should executions be bloody, excruciating, and public to fully inspire awe and "reverential fear"? Is it necessary to kill to show that killing is wrong? And, given the varied backgrounds and capacities of defendants, the diverse types of murder, and the limits of human understanding, is it even possible to decide fairly which murderers deserve to die?

The simplest counterargument is that, if killing is morally wrong, it is wrong for both the individual and the state. To be sure, there are circumstances where killing may be necessary, for example, when a police officer shoots a robber who is about to kill a clerk, when a soldier kills an enemy soldier during a time of war, when a woman shoots a violently abusive husband who is coming toward her brandishing a knife. These situations involve imminent danger, split-second decisions, and self-defense or defense of innocent others. Unlike police officers, who occasionally kill to protect their own lives or the lives of innocent people, the executioner performs an unnecessary killing, a killing that has nothing to do with self-defense, imminent danger, or the protection of society. The murderer has already been captured and waits in a prison cell safely isolated from the community.

The law of equal retribution proposed by Kant and others cannot be a literal prescription for how to punish violent criminals. We would find it morally repugnant to torture torturers, rape rapists, or terrorize terrorists. We do not try to kill murderers using the same method they used to kill their victims. Instead, we imprison them. Our efforts to mitigate punishments arise out the recognition that we must not sink to the level of the criminal; raping a rapist would debase us, weaken our moral solidarity, and undermine the moral authority of the state. We cannot simply respond to cruelty with our own acts of cruelty. Acts of brutality committed by the state in the name of justice never ennoble us. There must be severe punishment for horrible crimes, but that does not oblige us to kill those who have killed.

Try as we might, we can never sever the ties between moral concerns and practical realities. Morality can only be assessed in practice. Even if we accept the morality of the death penalty in the abstract, we must always look at how it is administered in the real world. Is the death penalty still moral if innocent people are sometimes convicted or executed? Is it still moral if the race of the victim or the murderer plays a substantial role in determining which defendants will be sentenced to die? Is it still moral if the ultimate penalty squanders money that could be more productively spent on preventing crime? Is it still moral if executions fail to deter violent criminals? These questions must be answered before any final judgment can be made about the morality of the death penalty. Moral theory cannot compensate for actual practice, and abstract benefits must be balanced against tangible costs. Defenders of capital punishment must defend this punishment *as it exists* in the real world.

Moral Responsibility and Free Will

Suppose a man has been convicted of a murder. In a jealous rage, he rapes his ex-wife and then stabs her to death. Clearly, he must be severely punished for his horrible crime. He has shown that he is violent, and society must be protected from him. His actions—rape and murder—legally qualify him for the death penalty. But before deciding whether he should die in the execution chamber or live out the rest of his life in prison, we must understand not only the crime, but also the criminal.

Here are four possibilities. First, suppose that he is a young man from a wealthy family who has enjoyed most of life's advantages: loving parents, material comfort, good schools, travel, and interesting experiences. Next, suppose that he is a young man with a brutal past: He and his mother suffered routine beatings from an abusive father throughout his childhood and into his adolescence. He grew up in a poverty-ridden, gang-infested neighborhood and received very little in the way of parental guidance or supervision. Third, suppose that he had an unremarkable middle-class background. He achieved his life's dream of becoming a Marine and was honored several times for his bravery. More than once he saved the lives of others. Or, finally, suppose that the killer is indisputably psychotic and that he had spent much of his life in mental institutions. He suffers from delusions and hallucinations, and he sincerely believed that his ex-wife was an alien disguised in human form who was about to commit a mass murder using advanced alien weapons.

The striking differences in the backgrounds of these men raise some disturbing questions. Are all four men equally deserving of death? Are all four equally responsible for their crimes? If not equally responsible, is one of them, say, 80% responsible, another 70%, 60%, or 50% responsible? Should background even matter? Does the good service of the Marine count for anything, or should all four men be treated the same? Would you be more inclined to show mercy if murderer number one was brain damaged? If murderer number two was a heroin addict?

Any assessment of moral blameworthiness must go beyond the act for which a person is on trial. All advanced systems of justice recognize this. That is not to say that the person's crime must be excused or that the person must not be severely punished. He must be held accountable, and there must be harsh consequences for his actions. It is merely to say that even identical crimes may have very different causes and may be the product of very different life circumstances. We judge, convict, and punish a person. And a person—even a person who has committed a hideous crime—is more than the worst thing he or she has ever done. We are obligated to look not only at the vicious act, but also to struggle to understand the circumstances that produced the act, the reasons and motives that lie beneath it.

Supporters of capital punishment would argue that this is precisely the kind of information jurors are instructed to consider when making the life-or-death decision. But the fact that jurors are told to take such information into account obscures the issue of our limited ability to understand the reasons behind someone else's actions. Imagine that you are a juror in a capital case. You have already decided that the defendant is guilty, and now you must decide whether he should be killed or sent to prison for the rest of his life. To decide whether to show mercy, you must attempt a full and fair assessment of the multitude of factors that led to the murder. To make this assessment, it is first necessary to have the defendant's important life events and experiences laid out before you: upbringing, family environment, education, formative experiences, the things that shaped his character and behavior. You would also need to know something about his inherited talents, abilities, and predilections. You would also need to have some understanding of how he responded to the events in his life, the impact of his experiences. You would also want to know about his mental state at the time of the crime, and you would want to know if he was cognitively impaired or suffering from a severe psychological disorder. Of course, it is impossible to know all of this. It is difficult enough to understand the behavior of people we have known for years. Even if we could manage to shut off our feelings of rage and revulsion, it would still be exceedingly difficult to find and consider enough information to allow us to fathom the reasons for a brutal murder. And, as a practical matter, no defense attorney has the time or resources to uncover or present all the necessary information. In addition, no judge will allow a capital trial to go on for months, and no set of jury instructions can adequately guide jurors in making this morally profound decision.

Despite scientific advances in psychological science and behavioral genetics, we are still a very long way from completely mapping out the motives, intentions, habits, interpretations, and situational pressures that propel a particular act of violence. The process is still somewhat mysterious. Perhaps if we had complete information and a year or two to sift through that information, we could arrive at a definitive answer to the question, "Why did this person commit this terrible crime?" But a thorough evaluation of moral culpability is clearly impossible within the constraints of the American courtroom. Some defenders present little information to help jurors, and even the most careful defenders and prosecutors cannot uncover and present all the reasons for the violent act. It is simply beyond human understanding. To believe that we can make such judgments is misguided hubris.

At the heart of the matter lies the ancient and difficult-to-resolve philosophical debate about whether behavior is determined or a function of free will. Without at least an assumption of free will, there can be no discussion of ethical behavior or criminal responsibility. Most of us believe in some measure of free will, but we are all partly determinists, too. Do you or do you not believe that you are a product of your genetic endowment and your life experiences? If you believe that your behavior is a function of inheritance and experience, you are at least what William James, the great philosopher and psychologist, might have called a "soft determinist." Whereas the "hard determinist" insists that our actions are entirely determined, that no one is free to act differently from the way he or she does act, the soft determinist believes that we possess free will within the constraints imposed by heredity and environment. That, although our actions are not fully determined, our actions are strongly influenced by our conditioning, our values and habits, and the situations we find ourselves in.

Especially over the past few decades, neuroscientists, psychologists, and philosophers have argued that free will is far more constrained than is commonly supposed (Gazzaniga, 2011; Harris, 2012). One strand of this argument is that every person's behavior is determined by their genetics and their environment. No one chooses their genetic endowment, and no one chooses their environment (at least during their formative childhood years). So, a large portion of who we are and who we are capable of becoming is predetermined by forces beyond our control. A second strand of the argument relies on experiments showing that the activity in the brain which indicates that a decision has been made *precedes* conscious awareness of that decision. That is, "the brain takes action before the mind decides" (Koch, 2012, p. 26). A third strand of the argument is that changes in brain chemistry—from a brain tumor, a disruption in neurotransmission, an imbalance of hormones, or degeneration of a brain structure—can produce criminal behaviors ranging from pedophilia to compulsive gambling to murder (Eagleman, 2011; Nestor, 2019). Such unchosen and involuntary biological changes can shift our cravings, warp our decision-making, intensify our emotions, and impair our capacity for self-restraint. Much of our legal system rests on the assumption that criminals choose to commit crimes. Even if free will is not entirely an illusion, the available research suggests that our ability to freely choose is heavily constrained. If criminals could not have acted differently than they did act, it does not make sense to construct a criminal justice system based on punishment and revenge. However, it does make sense to remove dangerous murderers from the rest of us by sentencing them to life without the possibility of parole (LWOP).

In discussing the reasons behind criminal behavior, Stephen Nathanson argues that we must take into account the effort required by a criminal to resist criminal actions and the obstacles to moral behavior encountered by the criminal.

> A person's degree of moral desert is determined by considerations of what could reasonably be expected of him. If a person faces such powerful obstacles to moral behavior that it would require extraordinary amounts of effort to act well, then, though he acts badly, he is not morally to blame ... different behavior could not reasonably be expected. The causes of difficulty need not be environmental. They could be physical, psychological, or of any sort, but if they make alternative actions extremely difficult or impossible, a person is not fully blameworthy for his deeds, even if they were wrong acts triggered by bad motives. (1987, p. 89)

The philosopher Jeffrey Reiman takes an even broader view, suggesting that the larger society must bear some responsibility for the actions of murderers. America spawns more vicious murderers than any other "civilized" country on Earth. The social conditions that predictably produce violent offenders (e.g., poverty, routine exposure to violence as a child, access to lethal weapons) are at least partly to blame. Put differently, every society bears some responsibility for violent criminals to the extent that it tolerates social conditions that predictably lead to violence. Until these conditions are remediated, some of the blame rests with the larger community (Reiman & Leighton, 2023).

The argument is not that murderers should be excused for their crimes. They must be held accountable and punished severely. The argument is that we cannot possibly fathom the multiple and subtle influences that caused a particular behavior. Instead of pretending to be omniscient, we should be humble about our ability to fully understand why someone commits a horrible crime. We can and should send a dangerous criminal to prison, but we should not presume to judge which people deserve to live and which deserve to die. Our judgments are bound to be faulty.

Just Revenge?

Beneath the usual justifications for punishing criminals lurks a more visceral and potent motive for the death penalty: revenge. The desire to lash back at those who have harmed us has deep roots in our evolutionary past. It is a powerful human motive that must be taken seriously, but it is not a sufficient justification for killing. Although individually we all feel the primitive urge to exact revenge against those who harm us, collectively we must strive to be more rational, fair, moral, and humane than the criminals who commit the acts of violence or cruelty that we condemn. We all sympathize with a bereaved father who attempts to kill the man who murdered his child. But a group's craving for revenge is far less innocent and immediate, and far less justifiable. A victim's relative who attempts to kill a murderer commits a crime of passion motivated by rage and grief. In contrast, the process leading up to a state-sponsored killing is slow, deliberate, methodical, and largely stripped of human emotion. The anger of the families of victims is understandable, but anger and the desire for revenge should not be the basis of social policy. As Sir Frances Bacon noted four centuries ago, "Revenge is a kind of wild justice; which the more man's nature runs to, the more ought law to weed it out."

We have all felt wronged and we have all experienced the powerful emotions that drive the hunger for revenge. The urge to see a murderer killed is rooted in the rage and revulsion that most of us feel when we hear about a horrible, inexplicable murder. We empathize with the victim and the family of the victim, and we want to see the murderer pay dearly for his or her crime. In movies, operas, plays, and novels, exacting revenge on those who offend us is often portrayed as cathartic and emotionally satisfying. But just because the appetite for revenge is real and powerful, that does not mean we should indulge our appetite or build it into our legal system. Justice must take precedence over revenge. Arthur Koestler made this point vividly: "Deep inside every civilized being there lurks a tiny Stone Age man, dangling a club to rob and rape, and screaming 'an eye for an eye.' But we would rather not have that little fur-clad figure dictate the law of the land" (Koestler, 1957, p. 101).

Feelings of anger and revulsion about a horrible crime are understandably human and maybe even an indication of concern for the welfare of others. However, even if we accept the legitimacy of anger, it does not mean that anger should outweigh all other considerations. Feelings of outrage and the quest for revenge do not guarantee that punishments will be fairly or rationally imposed. Anger does not ensure justice; it is an obstacle to justice.

It would be immoral to execute everyone who kills another human being. Every legal system on earth recognizes this. Consequently, every nation with capital punishment must create some method of selecting out those killers who truly "deserve" to die. Because no selection process is perfect, bias, prejudice, and error seep into every system of capital punishment. Too often, retentionists argue for the morality of the death penalty as it might exist in a theoretical, idealized world. But the claim that killing the killer is morally justified must be reconciled with disquieting facts: the inevitability of wrongful convictions, the reality of discrimination because of wealth and race, the certainty of convicting and executing innocent defendants, and the reality that millions of dollars must be squandered to bring about executions. Killing is a morally acceptable penalty only if it is essential and only if it provides substantial benefits that cannot be gained by any other means. Capital punishment is not just a moral abstraction. It is a reality that must be evaluated based on its actual costs and benefits.

What About the Victims?

Those who support the death penalty have a ready response to all arguments against it: "What about the victims?" The question is packed with implied meanings: that support for executions is based on selfless sympathy for the victims, that all families of victims of murder are entitled to (and find comfort in) the killing of the person convicted of murdering their loved one, that the abolitionists would be screaming for an execution if their loved ones had been brutally murdered. More fundamentally, the question is an attempt to control and restrict the terms of the debate. It is a demand that we choose sides—you must be either on the side of the victim and the victim's family or you must be on the side of the murderer. You must declare your allegiance: Are you pro-victim or pro-murderer?

If by killing a murderer we could resurrect the innocent victim, almost no one would oppose the death penalty. Unfortunately, there is nothing any of us can do to return the victim to the arms of his or her loved ones. The answer to the question, "What about the victim?" is not only that an execution will not restore the life of the victim; it is also that a state-sanctioned killing will debase us all and create a new set of victims: the murderer's family.

The wrenching loss of the victim's family cannot be fully appreciated by anyone who has not experienced it firsthand. Their suffering is unimaginable to most of us. The sudden, unexpected, violent death of a loved one has a profound and far-reaching impact (King, 2004; Vandiver, 2014). Whereas the loved ones of people who die from illness may have an opportunity to grieve in advance and to say their good-byes to the dying person, there are no such opportunities for the families of murder victims. When the death is caused not by a tragic accident but by the actions of a murderer, the shock and pain are amplified. The survivors must not only deal with their loss, but they must also find ways of dealing with feelings of rage and hatred for the murderer. The death creates disruptions in friendships, marriages, employment, physical health, and mental health. Many feel a sense of guilt and are haunted by intrusive recurring thoughts about what they might have done to prevent the murder (Pazzani, 2018). A murder also alters the worldview of the loved ones of the victim and can shatter their sense of security. As a woman whose grandchild was murdered put it, "The world is not good, it's evil and nobody is safe" (King, 2004, p. 203).

It is widely presumed that families of murder victims are uniformly in favor of executions and that execution of the murderer facilitates the healing process. These assumptions may sometimes be true. For example, after witnessing an execution, one relative of a murder victim described the event as therapeutic.

> It was spiritual. When he [the condemned man] leaned over for the last time, everything I went there for just lifted off my shoulders. I felt peace... I have finality.... It was like a miracle of forgiveness. (Wallace, 1992, p. A10)

Other family members of victims express the desire for the murderer to suffer ongoing torture instead of mere death. Some relatives of the victims of the notorious Golden State Killer (who killed thirteen people and raped more than fifty women) explained what they wanted to see happen to the serial killer/rapist:

> If I had my way, he would always be shivering and blindfolded; naked and exposed every moment from now on. He should be incarcerated in the toughest prison with the worst inmates. At least three or four nights a week he should be awakened by masked inmates with prison shanks. He should be bound, blindfolded, stripped, and forced to lay on a cold cell floor for two or three hours. His attackers would repeatedly rape him. . . . I wouldn't want to give him the easy way out. I would not want him to die. I would want these attacks to continue for the rest of his life. . . . I would want him to suffer for the rest of his life. (Greenblatt, 2020)

It is not uncommon for family members of murdered victims to prefer LWOP because they see the death penalty as "the easy way out" and they would prefer to see the convicted murderer suffer the harsher punishment of spending the rest of his life in prison. Many express the hope that during a prison sentence that lasts until he dies, the murderer will reflect on his actions and come to regret and repent what he has done (Bohm, 2013).

Journalists and prosecutors sometimes offer up the nebulous concept of "closure" to argue for executions rather than LWOP. The idea seems to be that only by killing the murderer can we enable victims to finally close the door on a horrible chapter of their lives and move on to the next chapter. But it is important to note that the vague, simplistic concept of closure does not correspond in any meaningful way to the long, complex, psychological process of grieving the death of a murdered loved one. Indeed, the primary sense in which closure seems to have meaning is in the sense of a closure of legal proceedings that require the ongoing attention of victim's families (Pazzani, 2018). When a capital defendant is sentenced to LWOP rather than death, legal proceedings end years if not decades sooner. Finally, if members of the victim's family "believed for years that the execution of their relative's killer would bring them substantial emotional relief and it does not, they may even feel worse after the execution" (Vandiver, 2014, p. 635). After witnessing the execution, one family member explained the experience this way: "There was no flood of relief. There was no lifting of weight, no sense of turning a personal page. . . . Remember, closure is for doors" (Berns, 2009, p. 392).

But the feelings and reactions of those who loved the victim are neither uniform nor predictable. For example, Coretta Scott King, who lost her husband (Dr. Martin Luther King, Jr.) and her mother-in-law to murder, said that,

> I stand firmly and unequivocally opposed to the death penalty for those convicted of capital offenses. An evil deed is not redeemed by an evil deed of retaliation. Justice is never advanced by the unnecessary taking of a human life. Morality is never upheld by legalized murder. (quoted in Tabak & Lane, 1989, p. 130)

Some survivors of murder victims have even actively fought to thwart the state's efforts to kill the person who murdered their loved one. There is at least one national organization—Murder Victims' Families for Reconciliation (MVFR)—comprised of people who have lost family members to violent crime but nonetheless advocate abolition of the death penalty. Their fundamental belief is that "healing happens not by vengeance but by reconciliation—with society, the community, the act of murder itself, and sometimes even with the offender." MVFR's founder, Marie Deans, posed the question, "How can we stand as murder victims, in our pain and sorrow, and give it to someone else's family as well?" She wrote,

> The hundreds of murder victims' families across the country who, to no avail, have pleaded for mercy for those who murdered their loved ones clearly demonstrate that the death penalty has nothing to do with the victims' families. . . . Victims' families simply serve as a cover-up for the fact that our leaders choose to gain votes by reacting to people's fears rather than by honestly responding to society's needs. (Kane, 1986, p. 34)

Odile Stern, former executive director of Parents of Murdered Children, opposes capital punishment and is "at peace" with the life sentence received by her daughter's murderer. She feels that the execution of a murderer "can never equate to the loss of your child's life and the horrors of murder" (Payton, 1997). Sam Reese Sheppard, whose pregnant mother was murdered when he was only seven years old, calls the death penalty "a hate crime" and believes that "it teaches that vengeance, hatred, and revenge are acceptable values to be cultivated and lived by our society" (Sheppard, 1995). Indeed, many relatives of murder victims show remarkable compassion and forgiveness.

> There is an old saying: "You would feel different if it happened to you." Well, it did happen to me. But after much thought and many tears I knew that my feelings on capital punishment had not changed. For I knew in my heart that killing is still wrong. . . . He must pay for what he did. But I don't wish him to be punished by death. (Kane, 1986)

For the families of most victims, the long, repetitive process of trials and appeals may retraumatize them and divert them from the task of trying to rebuild their devastated lives. The legal process leading up to an execution always consumes many years. Relatives who are determined to bring about an execution must devote a considerable amount of time and attention to the task. They must listen to countless descriptions of the murder; describe their grief in front of attorneys, judges, and maybe even television cameras; and wait for years while the overburdened legal system makes a final determination. And even if the execution finally comes, they still must go on without their loved one. The long, slow process of trials and appeals (which often require decades of involvement by the victim's family) unnecessarily prolongs the terrible suffering created by a murder. Healing and recovery, according to the National Organization of Victim Assistance, come from "an increased remembrance of the victim—not the murder." The police investigations, trials, appeals, clemency hearings, and meetings with legal personnel repeatedly dredge up terrible memories. Such events may prolong the mourning process and offer little relief from the pain of loss (Lifton & Mitchell, 2002).

The Families of the Murderers

There is a secondary, seldom-considered set of victims: the murderer's family. A sentence of death creates additional suffering for the family of the condemned prisoner. The convict is always someone's son, and he is often a brother, a husband, or a father. The relatives of the condemned prisoner— who are often innocent of any wrongdoing—are swept into the widening circle of suffering created by a killing and a counterkilling. Mothers, fathers, sisters, brothers, spouses, and children wait for their loved one to be strapped down and killed by the state. In his moving book, *Shot in the Heart*, Mikal Gilmore describes the pain caused by the execution of his brother Gary.

> One moment you're forcing yourself to live through the hell of knowing that somebody you love is going to die in a known way, at a specific time and place, and that not only is there nothing you can do to change that, but that for the rest of your life, you will have to move around in a world that wanted this death to happen. You will have to walk past people every day who were heartened by the killing of somebody in your family—somebody who had long ago been himself murdered emotionally. You will have to live in this world and either hate it or make peace with it, because it is the only world you will have available to live in. (Gilmore, 1994, p. 349)

The shame and stigma of being related to someone on death row is painfully felt by the families of the condemned: "I've found that people can be very cruel when they learn you have an immediate family member on death row. Generally, they leave you with the impression they think you are tainted because you are related to a convicted killer" (Kane, 1986, p. 35). Albert Camus made the point eloquently.

> The relatives of the condemned man then discover an excess of suffering that punishes them beyond all justice. A mother's or father's long months of waiting, the visiting-room, the artificial conversations filling up the brief moments spent with the condemned man, the visions of the execution are all tortures. (1960, p. 205)

Families of the condemned and families of the victim share an experience that is similar in some respects.

> The homicide victim dies by sudden, passionate, individual violence, while the condemned prisoner dies by slow, deliberate, and collective violence. The survivors of both must live with the knowledge that their relative died from the intentional acts of others. (Vandiver, 2014, p. 128)

Studies of the families of death row inmates reveal an agonizing mix of emotions: They feel angry that so many people want to see their loved one killed and they become acutely sensitive to how others view the impending execution; they swing between hope and despair as the appeals process progresses; they engage in self-recrimination about what they might have done to prevent the murder; they may be haunted by obsessive thoughts about the murder and the execution to come; they grieve in anticipation of the execution; they worry about the enduring impact the eventual execution will have on them and other family members, especially children (Sharp, 2005).

The condemned man's family must live with the loss of someone they love. They must also live with the humiliation and stigma of being related to a person deemed so vile that he had to be exterminated. One mother of a man sentenced to death reported that, "Most people just flat out said that I had raised the devil himself. This came from friends, family, and complete strangers" (Sharp, 2005, p. 62). Other families suffered harassment— threatening phone calls, online harassment, killed pets, and flattened car tires. An execution may or may not bring solace to the victim's family, but it surely enlarges the scope of suffering to include the murderer's family.

The Famous Few

It is essential to keep in mind that even in years when executions are relatively frequent, fewer than 1% of murderers end up in the execution chamber. The other 99% of victim's families must content themselves with a sentence less than death. Because of this fact, the existence of the death penalty creates yet another problem: Some families will feel cheated because the person who murdered their loved one will never be sent to the execution chamber. Still other families feel cheated if the murderer *is* killed. Jeffrey Dahmer—serial killer and subject of several documentaries—was sentenced to life imprisonment for a hideous string of killings. But after serving only a couple years of his sentence, he was murdered by another inmate. The mother of one of Dahmer's victims was disappointed by his death. "It's not fair," she said. "His suffering is over now but we will suffer for the rest of our lives." Instead of executing a tiny percentage of murderers, we could choose to spend some of the money now spent on capital punishment to provide emotional and financial assistance to the survivors of murder victims.

There is another sense in which executions don't serve the interests of the victim's family. Executions often bestow celebrity status on the condemned prisoner and draw attention away from the victims. The victim's survivors often feel betrayed by the courts and the media. You no doubt know the names of some of the worst serial killers, and you may even know the name of some condemned murderer who was recently executed in your state. But do you know the names of their victims? As the execution date approaches, a condemned man often becomes the object of sympathy. After all, he is about to be deliberately killed by the state in a carefully premeditated ritual at a specific, predetermined time. Many of the worst murderers seem to enjoy the most notoriety, and their fame often surges as their execution day approaches. While waiting on death row, the prolific serial killer John Wayne Gacy produced oil paintings that were exhibited in New York and Los Angeles. He had his own phone number where callers could pay to listen to a recorded twelve-minute statement by Gacy. Paintings and books of poetry by death row prisoners can be purchased online, streaming services offer a rich collection of documentaries about serial killers, and each execution is accompanied by a flurry of publicity.

Reporters and commentators are irresistibly drawn to executions, and a significant segment of the American public is morbidly fascinated by the details of the murders, by the life of the murderer, and by the ritual of the execution. It is a tantalizing media opportunity: the drama of last-minute legal maneuvering, the countdown to the killing, the last meal, the killer's final hours and last words, the reaction of the victim's family, the crowds of protestors and supporters chanting and carrying signs outside the prison, and the possibility of a bungled execution. Since the days of public hangings, it has never been otherwise. Some portion of the public will always display a depraved curiosity about murderers and executions. The only way to wipe away this ugly sensationalism is to dismantle our execution chambers.

9

The Slow Death of Capital Punishment
in the United States

DEATH SENTENCES AND EXECUTIONS ARE both in decline. Over the past ten years, we have sent about forty new inmates to death row per year, and, during the same period, we have executed about twenty-two prisoners each year. The incoming residents of death row are added to the roughly 2,300 people who are already living there. Most death row inmates will not die at the hands of the executioner. Some will have their convictions overturned, many will have their sentences changed to life imprisonment without parole, many more will die of natural causes. These numbers expose our current system of capital punishment as little more than an elaborate, cruel, and costly charade.

Ironically, if the floodgates were thrown open and hundreds of prisoners were killed in a year, it would probably only hasten the demise of capital punishment. We would see frequent accounts in the media of state-sanctioned shootings, electrocutions, and lethal injections. The men strapped down in the execution chamber would be poor, disproportionately dark-skinned, and most of their crimes would be indistinguishable from those of many others who were given life sentences. Some would be innocent. Americans would be forced to confront the death penalty as a practice rather than as an abstraction. Political candidates would no longer be able to simply pledge their allegiance to the death penalty. They would have to defend capital punishment with all its costs, contradictions, and consequences.

Abstract support for killing murderers has also declined (see Chapter 4), and our ambivalence about executions seems to restrain us from executing most of the prisoners sentenced to death. For now, we can hide from the ugly realities of how death sentences are handed down and carried out. Our current system of infrequent executions allows us to preserve the symbolism of capital punishment without having to witness a killing spree. Despite all the political bluster about being tough on crime, most politicians seem to understand that generalized support for the death penalty does not translate into public enthusiasm for frequent executions. Moreover, clearing the road to the execution chamber would require a massive infusion of resources, not just political posturing.

A mostly idle execution chamber allows supporters of capital punishment to occasionally see the performance of a grand morality play: a despicable murderer is killed by the state using modern "humane" methods. Good triumphs over evil. Unfortunately, the actors often spoil the drama by failing to follow the assigned script. The execution takes place decades after the conviction, investigations of the murderer's life reveal a shocking history of neglect and abuse, the murderer claims to be innocent, the relatives of the victim don't want an execution, the execution is botched, the murderer suffers from mental illness or is brain-damaged or intellectually impaired. The show must still go on, but the moral of the story is tainted.

Other Western Democracies

When we attempt to evaluate life in America, we compare ourselves to other industrialized democracies—Australia, Canada, England, New Zealand, and all of Western Europe. We look to these countries to see how we measure up on education, healthcare, economic productivity, and quality of life. We prefer to be in the company of other advanced, enlightened countries that value human rights. But when it comes to the death penalty, the United States stands alone. Countries that share our cultural traditions have abolished it outright, or they reserve it for treason or wartime crimes. Most of the countries in Central and South America—Argentina, Bolivia, Brazil, Colombia, Costa Rica, Ecuador, El Salvador, Mexico, Nicaragua, Panama, Paraguay, Peru, Uruguay, and Venezuela—have also abandoned capital punishment or they permit it only for extraordinary crimes. Many countries refuse to extradite criminals to the United States if they might be eligible for the death penalty, and some countries donate money and legal aid to their citizens who face execution in the United States. By clinging to capital punishment, we place ourselves in the company of some of the cruelest and most repressive governments in the world: China, Iraq, Iran, Libya, and North Korea. Our continued use of killing as a form of punishment undermines our credibility when we advocate for human rights in other countries.

In 1995, South Africa closed another door to its repressive past by declaring the death penalty unconstitutional. Like many other countries, Germany and Italy among them, South Africa's experience with severe political repression helped to bring an end to capital punishment. Germany adopted a constitution that prohibited use of the death penalty after World War II. The Nazis had provided a horrific demonstration of how the power to kill could be used by governments. In the past fifty years, only two countries—Argentina and Brazil—have reinstated the death penalty. These reinstatements occurred after military coups and were followed by re-abolition of the death penalty when the countries returned to democracies (Hood & Hoyle, 2009). Brutal regimes always rely on the death penalty to solidify their power. One reason why execution chambers still exist in America is that the United States has not experienced executions as an overt means of state oppression.

In most democracies, the death penalty is viewed as a basic human rights issue: Governments should not be granted the power to kill their own citizens except in rare cases of absolute necessity. When capital punishment is legal, there is always the possibility of abuse, a temptation to rely on killing as a solution to political problems. And there is always the likelihood of biased and discriminatory use of executions. Opposition to the death penalty and support for human rights rely on the same underlying conception of the proper relationship between governments and individual citizens. That conception emphasizes restraints on the power of governments to deprive individual citizens of life or liberty for political ends.

A second glaring difference between the United States and other democracies is that our legal system is far more decentralized. Much of the criminal justice system is within the jurisdiction of individual states, so each state can choose whether to retain or abandon capital punishment. As noted earlier, in recent years, about 85% of executions have been carried out in just five states: Texas, Oklahoma, Missouri, Alabama, and Florida. These states fought vigorously to reinstate capital punishment in 1976, and, if the issue is left to the states, they will probably be among the last to allow the practice of killing to die out. Yet despite state authority, the death penalty is still a national issue: questions about human rights, morality, cruelty, cost, and fairness cross all state lines.

The Fading Political Power of the Death Penalty

The death penalty survives because there are benefits associated with it. But the benefits are shrinking, and the costs are rising. Two groups receive some benefit from the death penalty: the public and the politicians. For the public, the benefits are largely symbolic and illusory. Capital punishment enables citizens to vent their anger toward violent criminals, express frustration with the impotence of the criminal justice system, and satisfy the craving for revenge. Anger and fear energize public support for capital punishment. Social psychologists remind us that "anger is the most positive of the negative emotions because it is the only one that confers a sense of power. When politicians argue, angrily, for the death penalty, they may communicate that they are in control, and at the same time arouse a satisfying sense of outrage and power in the voter" (Ellsworth & Gross, 1994). Although an occasional execution may be emotionally satisfying for some Americans and inspire a false sense of control for others, this benefit is purchased at a very high price.

For politicians, the payoff has been more tangible and immediate. By declaring support for capital punishment, ambitious politicians have been able to quickly portray themselves as tough on crime. Historically, the issue of capital punishment has been a key issue in presidential elections and state gubernatorial races. Along with other symbolic issues, a candidate's position on the death penalty has often been used to quickly define candidates to voters. Many politicians have enthusiastically embraced the death penalty and some have even proposed that its use be expanded to a host of new crimes. And, in the United States, the death penalty is politicized at the lowest level—the trial level. Prosecutors and judges are elected in most states. For prosecutors who want to become judges, the publicity surrounding a capital murder trial can propel their political careers. They can be seen as an anti-crime warrior locked in a struggle to send a vicious murderer to his death.

Although all but the most courageous politicians are skittish about proposing alternatives to the death penalty, survey research reveals a broad receptiveness to alternative punishments for murderers. Among the citizenry, there is a deep ambivalence about the death penalty. Juries are hesitant to impose it, and most Americans recognize that discrimination, inequity, and error are an inherent part of the system that sends some prisoners to their deaths. While there is no doubt that Americans want punishment for and protection from murderers, that does not mean that the public will settle only for killing. Politicians have misread or purposely ignored the polls. Americans appear to favor the death penalty only if the alternative is life imprisonment *with* the possibility of parole.

The fight over capital punishment has launched and scuttled political careers. Americans usually place violent crime near the top of their lists of concerns, and often the political rhetoric surrounding violent crime is as superheated as it is superficial. Politicians are faced with a dilemma. In a ten-second sound bite they can declare their allegiance to the death penalty and show that they are angry about violent offenders. The argument for abolition takes more time and is more complex. A public declaration of opposition to the death penalty is too often seen as damaging, or perhaps even fatal, to a candidacy. In the abstract, the execution chamber is a shining symbol of America's resolve to deal decisively with violent criminals. Politicians gain a potent political weapon in exchange for pretending—in the face of massive evidence to the contrary—that the death penalty can be made to be effective and just. In the war on crime, abolition has often been portrayed as unilateral disarmament.

The policy of capital punishment costs more than just taxpayer dollars and court time. It has a huge social cost: It commandeers and corrupts our national debate over crime and punishment. It lets politicians off the hook. Meanwhile, politicians breathe a sigh of relief because they no longer need to propose detailed solutions or engage in a searching debate about how to prevent and respond to violence. Productive discussions about the social conditions that spawn violent crime (e.g., poverty, hopelessness, unemployment, domestic violence, access to firearms) or about effective responses to violence (e.g., enhanced crime detection, certainty of apprehension, rehabilitation, restitution, and alternatives to incarceration) are displaced by facile declarations of support for capital punishment. Executions thus become a sideshow designed to divert attention from the crisis in center ring: Although the death penalty appears to be a form of decisive action, it is merely a mask for inaction, an attempt to conceal failure.

The violent crime rate in the United States has declined substantially over the past thirty years, but it is still much higher than rates in other advanced democracies. A probing debate about how to prevent and reduce violent crime is desperately needed. Instead, by focusing on the executions of a few individual murderers, we divert precious attention and resources from treating the causes of crime. Constructive reforms that carry the potential to reduce violent crime remain untried or are quickly abandoned. While educational programs, family support services, early intervention, and treatment programs must fight for funding, billions are squandered to preserve the penalty of death.

The death penalty is public property. We own it. Executions are carried out in our names, at our expense. Our political leaders owe us full disclosure of its costs and consequences. It is irresponsible to be willfully ignorant of how it is administered or to deliberately ignore the troubling realities of error and discrimination. Eventually, realities must take precedence over magical thinking. If a policy harms public safety, wastes taxpayer money, and systematically discriminates, elected representatives are ethically obliged to change or abandon that policy.

The Role of the Media

Despite the high murder rate in the United States, few Americans are murderers, or victims of murder, or friends and family of either group. Thankfully, for most of us, murder is a terrifying but remote possibility. Because of this lack of personal experience with murder, most Americans rely on the mass media for information about its prevalence. In many studies, Americans vastly overestimate murder rates, and this effect is especially strong for frequent TV viewers (Gramlich, 2022).

This is not surprising. The mass media pours out a steady stream of violence. Any time of the day or night, we can turn on our TVs and laptops and watch dramas about thugs, perverts, rapists, terrorists, and serial killers. The simplified and stereotyped portrayals of crime in fictional programs and in newscasts create deep misconceptions and great fear. As fear and anxiety grow, the public becomes increasingly receptive to any policy that has even a remote chance of pushing back the perceived tidal wave of violence. It is at this point that the media and politicians enter into a destructive partnership: The fear instilled by the media is soothed by politicians who propose the death penalty as a simple and decisive solution to violent crime.

The death penalty is the triumph of symbolism over realism. But just because public support is largely symbolic, it does not mean that hearts and minds cannot be swayed by new, compelling information. Attitudes are resistant to change but they are not unchangeable. As information about the costs and consequences of the death penalty has become more widely publicized, there has been a sizable shift in public support. Still, for the most part, the mainstream media confines its coverage of the death penalty to executions and political campaigns. Expanded coverage tends to be reserved for botched executions or executions involving infamous murderers. It is simply not the kind of coverage that stimulates probing discussions.

The Alternative to Killing

Some people argue that murderers should be killed because they might harm or kill inmates or prison personnel. After all, murderers have already been convicted of vicious crimes, and, since they will never be released from prison, they have nothing to lose. Therefore, it is best to execute them. While it is true that a corpse can't commit further crimes, there is no evidence to suggest that inmates serving life sentences for murder are any more dangerous than the general prison population (Prescott et al., 2020; Sorensen & Reidy, 2019). Inmates vary in their adaptation to prison. Some murderers continue to be dangerous in prison; others are tamed and broken by the experience. Many murderers are weak men who pulled a trigger during the commission of a robbery. Once they are placed in a prison cell, they no longer pose a threat (Johnson & Dobrzanska, 2005). The converse is also true: Some who enter prison for nonviolent offenses become murderous while in prison. Although well-publicized serial murders come easily to mind, very few murderers kill more than once. Indeed, there is evidence to suggest that "lifers" are better behaved than the general prison population and may even have a stabilizing influence on other inmates (Leigey, 2015; Wooldredge, 2020). Lifers, like any other inmates, can be disciplined for any violation of rules. They can be confined to their cell, placed in isolation, and/or their minimal privileges can be revoked. Lifers recognize that prison will always be their only home. Most strive to create a predictable, secure environment because there is no prospect of release and there are heavy penalties for misbehavior. Past behavior on the outside is simply not a reliable predictor of behavior in prison. In a system without capital punishment, local prison administrators would be granted greater latitude to decide which prisoners should be placed in the limited number of high-security cells.

There is a simple solution to the myriad of problems created by the death penalty: Abolish the death penalty. But what would happen to convicted murderers if there were no more executions? There is already a realistic alternative to killing them: life imprisonment without parole (LWOP). If we tore down the execution chambers, people convicted of what are now capital crimes would receive an automatic sentence of LWOP.

A sentence of LWOP has several advantages over a sentence of death. First, it takes effect as soon as the sentence is handed down. When no execution is at stake, the number of appeals is vastly reduced. Second, the community can rest assured that the murderer's fate is sealed, and the victim's loved ones can begin to rebuild their devastated lives. Third, the convict sinks into the anonymity of a gray penitentiary instead of becoming a tragic figure battling to foil the state's efforts to kill him. Finally, LWOP is a harsh punishment by any measure. Perhaps some people feel that a life spent in prison is too lenient a punishment for killers. A little imagination and a visit to any overcrowded American penitentiary should be sufficient to dispel that misconception. Murderers sentenced to LWOP suffer all the pains of prison life: a bleak, barren environment; loss of control over all but the most trivial decisions; loss of contact with family and friends; crushing boredom; and a grinding fear of other inmates and prison guards. This sense of fear and vulnerability only grows as the prisoner ages and the prison fills up with younger, stronger inmates. All this without any hope of release. LWOP is the death penalty in passive form: God or fate, not the state, decides when the inmate will die in prison.

Because jurors are reluctant to impose a death sentence, and because a substantial number of death sentences are vacated on appeal, an LWOP sentence would be swifter, surer, and more final. The uniquely long and complex process of capital appeals would not be necessary. There would also be far more equity: Everyone convicted of aggravated murder would receive the same punishment regardless of race or wealth. Mistakes would still occur (although the probability of uncovering mistakes would be much higher), but we would never again kill the wrong person or torture someone with the threat of execution.

Once the death penalty is abandoned, LWOP will become the maximum available sentence. This would be a great step forward for our criminal justice system. However, it is worth noting that the United States would still be out of step with nearly all other advanced democracies, who do hand down very long sentences (e.g., forty years), but do not have LWOP as an option. Just like our current death penalty system, which holds people in prison until they die and executes a small number of them, LWOP requires prisons to hold on to convicted murderers even if they are elderly, disabled, or suffering from dementia. Although few Americans realize it, our prisons are increasingly in the business of healthcare as prisoners in their sixties, seventies, and eighties begin to suffer the health declines associated with aging. LWOP (just like the death penalty) requires that prisons are partly medical geriatric care facilities. Among states that have already abandoned capital punishment, there are already wide-ranging discussions about alternatives to LWOP. In a post–death penalty country, a more thorough evaluation of the effectiveness of all sentencing options finally becomes possible.

Toward Abolition

As societies evolve, the death penalty is applied to an increasingly narrow range of crimes. Eventually, it is used only for the most egregious crimes, such as felony murder or multiple murder, and later it is used only for "extraordinary crimes" (e.g., treason or terrorism). Finally, it is abolished. Although it is impossible to predict how and when America will abandon the death penalty, some scenarios seem more likely than others.

It is unlikely that the current Supreme Court will rule that the death penalty is unconstitutional. Prior to the addition of three extremely conservative justices by former President Trump, many commentators seemed hopeful that the Court might soon rule the death penalty unconstitutional (e.g., Bookman, 2021; Garrett, 2017). That hope has now dimmed. If the court was so inclined, it could find abundant evidence of discrimination and arbitrariness in death sentencing, strong evidence that executions do not deter potential murderers, and ample public opinion evidence that the death penalty offends contemporary standards of fairness. All this evidence is far more compelling than it was at the time of *Furman v. Georgia*. But for now, the majority of Justices show no inclination to be moved by such evidence.

An additional problem is the Court's inability and unwillingness to understand complex statistical analyses. Historically, the Court has been willing to engage in elaborate rhetorical contortions to resist and then dismiss any sophisticated statistical evidence that the penalty is administered in an unconstitutional manner. But even though the Justices have difficulty understanding probabilities, significance levels, and effect sizes, they do know how to count. And counting has been a major means of assessing whether the death penalty is still consistent with "the evolving standards of decency that mark the progress of a maturing society." If we simply count the number of states that retain the death penalty, there has been a steady decline—at present, twenty-three states have abolished the death penalty and six more have a governor-imposed moratorium. Only one state

(Nebraska) has reinstated capital punishment in the past thirty years. If three of the states with moratoria move to full abolition, a bare majority of states will have no death penalty. Such a circumstance should allow inclined members of the Court to conclude that executions are incompatible with "evolving standards of decency." Indeed, in both *Atkins v. Virginia* and *Roper v. Simmons*, the Supreme Court used a state-counting method to exclude juvenile and intellectually impaired defendants from being sentenced to death. When *Atkins* was decided, eighteen states had already prohibited the execution of "mentally retarded persons," and, at the time of *Roper*, twelve states had already abolished the death penalty and another eighteen had already prohibited it for juveniles. Other simple indices of "evolving standards of decency" could also be used by the Court to support abolition. For example, the yearly number of executions has fallen steadily since it peaked at ninety-eight in 1999. During the five-year period from 2000 to 2004, the number of executions per year averaged 69.2. For 2005–2009, that yearly average had declined to 48.8. From 2010 to 2014, the yearly average was 41.2, and from 2015 through 2019, it was 23.6. Since 2020, the yearly average is 17.5.

There is also strong evidence of a developing international consensus against use of the death penalty. More than 70% of countries in the world have abolished capital punishment or no longer use it (Death Penalty Information Center [DPIC], 2024). As mentioned earlier, all the Western democracies we habitually compare ourselves to in standard of living, quality of life, democratic values, and human rights are abolitionist. Moreover, a variety of international organizations—including the United Nations, the International Criminal Court, the European Union, and the Organization of American States—have adopted policies prohibiting executions.

For now, the Supreme Court has chosen to abdicate its moral authority and defer to state legislatures. But the strong and consistent evidence of discrimination, error-proneness, and arbitrary application of the death penalty cannot be pushed aside forever. Eventually, through turnover in Supreme Court Justices or by a change in the minds or hearts of a few of the current Justices, the death penalty could be declared unconstitutional once again. Because it is both powerful and politically insulated, the Supreme Court may still be the best hope for full, national abolition.

There is a slower, less direct road to abolition—the death penalty could be abandoned in a piecemeal fashion, state by state. We have been traveling down this meandering road for more than a decade. In 2021, the Governor of Virginia signed a bill making his state the twenty-third to abolish the death penalty. This event was especially notable because Virginia is in the South, and, historically, it had been one of the states that carried out the most executions. A decade ago, abolition in a state like Virginia would have been an incendiary event. But in 2021, there was only a muted backlash. Times have changed.

It is not that the newly abolitionist states have experienced moral epiphanies; instead, they are responding to a more mundane set of concerns. Chief among these concerns is the crushing cost of capital punishment to states and counties. But there are other factors at play, including sagging public support, the reduced ability of prosecutors to secure sentences of death, and well-publicized wrongful convictions. It is possible that our system of capital punishment may slowly collapse, state-by-state, under its own weight. Political leadership could help tip the scales sooner. The US president and state governors, as well as human rights, medical, legal, and religious organizations, could help exert the moral leadership that might shorten the road to abolition.

The Message We Send

Much of the appeal of the death penalty lies in symbolism. But what message is sent by occasionally killing a killer? Killing is an odd way to show that killing is wrong, and an odd way to show that our society is just and humane. We intend to send the message that murderers will be killed and thereby deter people who are contemplating murder. We also intend to get revenge. Yet, despite our intentions, we send the message that killing is an acceptable way of solving the problem of violence and that a killer's life should be extinguished if we have the power. We lend legal authority to the dangerous idea that if someone has committed a depraved crime, we should treat him or her as a person who can be killed without remorse.

We could choose to react differently. We could refuse to respond to killers with a killing of our own. An execution is an endorsement of revenge, a statement that fear and anger ought to be granted full expression. Blinded by the urge for revenge, we support a corrupt system of punishment. To preserve the primitive satisfaction gained from killing the occasional murderer, we must be willing to tolerate an arbitrary, costly, discriminatory system that sometimes kills an innocent person. Renunciation of the death penalty would send a clearer, more constructive message: That we will not debase ourselves by killing, that the government should not have the power to kill its citizens, and that we are willing to forsake eye-for-an-eye revenge in favor of a fairer, less expensive, more humane alternative.

In part, the death penalty is a response to fear and social turbulence. As a leading scholar pointed out long ago, "It flourished in America with the institution of slavery, with racial strife during Reconstruction, and with economic adversity at the time of the Great Depression, especially in the regions where these conditions were most keenly felt" (Bowers et al., 1984, p 385). When the fear of violence is high or rising, executions reassure us that we are at least doing something. The morality play of trial and execution enables the public to believe that our legal system is, at least occasionally, capable of taking decisive action. The public ritual of arrest, conviction, sentencing, and execution is meant to reassure the public and give expression to their anger. Unfortunately, the reality is that instead of protecting society and serving the ideal of justice, the death penalty harms public safety and contributes to injustice.

We do not allow executions to be streamed live on TV or the internet. The spectacle of televised executions would offend our collective sensibilities as a civilized people and expose executions as shameful and anachronistic rituals. The solution we endorse in the abstract is less appealing when it becomes a flesh-and-blood matter. When we kill a prisoner, we do it with only a small group of witnesses looking on. Few are allowed to see the prisoner strapped in, few get to see the needles inserted in his arms, few get to watch him die, few get to view the corpse. We take pains to hide the identity of the executioners, and we conduct the killing in an isolated wing of the prison. We have even tried to make the act of killing as palatable and "painless" as possible. Executions are designed to be passionless, bureaucratic rituals stripped of anger or excitement. They are the most methodical, cold-blooded, premeditated form of killing. To soothe any pangs of conscience, we remind ourselves of what the murderer did, and, as the rage and revulsion rise up in us, we once again feel that executions might be justified.

The influential anthropologist Bronislaw Malinowski argued that cultures turn to magic when knowledge and reason fail (Malinowski, 1954). Other anthropologists have pointed out that executions are not unlike ancient human sacrifices. Both are wrapped in ritual. For executions there is the last supper, the reading of the death warrant, the last walk, the visit with clergy, and the weighing and measuring of the doomed man. But the most fundamental similarity between an execution and a human sacrifice is that both are irrational attempts to alter mysterious and frightening forces, attempts by state officials to demonstrate that they are still in control. The killing of prisoners persists not because it stems the tide of violent crime, but because, like human sacrifice, it creates the comforting illusion that the state is taking decisive action. Executions are acts of desperation, admissions of failure. Like human sacrifices, executions do not appease the gods, ward off the forces of evil, or restore social order. After the corpse has been carried from the execution chamber, we are no safer and we are less civilized.

The United States is still bucking the worldwide trend toward abolition, a trend that is especially strong in open, democratic societies where there are ample opportunities to debate the utility and morality of different criminal sanctions. There is a strong, though not steady, tendency for punishments to become less harsh as societies evolve and moral sensibilities mature. Social upheaval, rising crime rates, or political demagoguery can slow, but not halt, this progress. Eventually, torture, killing, and the infliction of unnecessary suffering come to be seen as morally wrong. As societies mature, punishments are evaluated on the criteria of effectiveness, humaneness, and fairness of application, not on hollow symbolism.

In Conclusion

Capital punishment is a failed social policy. It is clearly time to abandon this relic of the barbaric past. Killing was once a brutal public spectacle designed to terrify the masses and to demonstrate the fearsome power of the state. Today, we would find such spectacles vile and repugnant. If we want to be seen as a truly civilized country, we should not permit premeditated legal killing. No legal system can decide who should live or die in a way that is unbiased and infallible. We should not pretend otherwise. Support for the death penalty rests on a sort of unthinking sentimentality. It requires a belief that legal killings will magically suppress illegal killings, a willingness to ignore the massive costs of our death penalty system, and an irrational faith in the legal system's ability to discern those who should die without prejudice or error. Most of all, it requires that we turn away from the facts and stubbornly refuse to look back.

REFERENCES

ABA (2023). "Death Penalty Policies." https://www.americanbar.org/groups/com mittees/ deathpenaltyrepresentation/resources/dp-policy/

Abbott, G. (1991). *Lords of the Scaffold*. New York: St. Martin's Press.

Abbott, J. (October 20, 2009). "Death Penalty Not a Deterrent, Police Chiefs Say." *The Columbus Dispatch*. https://www.dispatch.com/story/news/2009/10/20/ death-penalty-not-deterrent-police/23848753007/

Abu-Jamal, M. (1995). *Live from Death Row*. Reading, MA: Addison-Wesley.

Allen, S. (August 6, 2016). "Majority of Oklahomans Support Replacing Death Penalty with Life Sentences, Poll Shows." *The Oklahoman*. https://www.oklaho man.com/majority-of-oklahomans-support-replacing-death-penalty-with-life-sentences-poll-shows/article/5512693/

Amnesty International (1989). *When the State Kills*. New York: Amnesty International USA.

Amnesty International (1995). *The Machinery of Death*. New York: Amnesty International USA.

Amnesty International (2023). "Global Report: Death Sentences and Executions." Amnesty International USA. https://www.amnesty.org/en/documents/act50/ 6548/2023/en/

Amnesty International (2023). Torture. https://www.amnesty.org/en/what-we-do/ torture/

Amsterdam, A. G. (1982). "Capital Punishment." In H. Bedau, ed., *The Death Penalty in America*, 346–358. New York: Oxford University Press.

Andersen, K. (January 24, 1983). "An Eye for an Eye." *Time*, 28–39.

Andone, D., D. Royal, & A. Spells (November 2, 2022). "Parkland School Shooter Sentenced to Life in Prison Without Parole for 2018 Massacre." CNN. https://

www.cnn.com/2022/11/02/us/parkland-shooter-nikolas-cruz-sentencing-wednesday/index.html

Andrews, W. (1991). *Old Time Punishments.* New York: Dorset Press.

Antonio, M. E. (2008). "Stress and the Capital Jury: How Male and Female Jurors React to Serving on a Murder Trial." *Justice System Journal* 29, 396–407.

Archer, D., & R. Gartner (1984). *Violence and Crime in Cross-National Perspective.* New Haven, CT: Yale University Press.

Atkins v. Virginia (2002).536 U.S. 304.

Bailey, W. (1990). "Murder, Capital Punishment, and Television: Execution Publicity and Homicide Rates." *American Sociological Review* 55, 628–633.

Bailey, W. C., & R. D. Peterson (1987). "Police Killings and Capital Punishment: The Post-Furman Period." *Criminology* 25, 1–25.

Bailey, W. C., & R. D. Peterson (1994). "Murder, Capital Punishment and Deterrence: A Review of the Evidence and an Examination of Police Killings." *Journal of Social Issues* 50, 53–74.

Baldus, D. C., & J. W. Cole (1975). "Statistical Evidence on the Deterrent Effect of Capital Punishment: A Comparison of the Work of Thorsten Sellin and Isaac Ehrlich." *Yale Law Journal* 85, 170–186.

Barclay v. Florida (1983). 463 US 939.

Baldus, D.C., C.M. Grosso, G. Woodworth, & R. Newell (2012). "Racial Discrimination in the Administration of the Death Penalty: The Experience of the United States Armed Forces (1984-2005)." *Journal of Crime. Law. & Criminology* 101, 1227–1335. http://www.jstor.org/stable/23150017

Baldus, D.C., C. Pulaski, & G. Woodworth (1983). "Comparative Review of Death Sentences: An Empirical Study of the Georgia Experience." *Journal of Criminal Law & Criminology* 74 (3), 661–753.

Baldus, D.C., & G. Woodworth (2003). "Race Discrimination and the Death Penalty: An Empirical and Legal Overview." In J.R. Acker, R.M. Bohm, & Lanier, eds., *America's Experiment with Capital Punishment*, 501–551. Durham, NC: Carolina Academic Press.

Baldus, D.C., G. Woodworth, & C. A. Pulaski Jr. (1985). "Monitoring and Evaluating Contemporary Death Sentencing Systems: Lessons from Georgia." *University of California Davis Law Review* 18, 1375–1407.

Baldus, D.C., G.G. Woodworth, & C.A. Pulaski (1990). *Equal Justice and the Death Penalty.* Boston: Northeastern University Press.

Barner, J. R. (2014). "Life or Death Decision Making: Qualitative Analysis of Death Penalty Jurors." *Qualitative Social Work* 13 (6), 842–858.

Baumgartner, F., C. Caron, & S. Duxbury (2023). "Racial Resentment and the Death Penalty." *Journal of Race, Ethnicity, and Politics* 8 (1), 42–60. https://doi.org/10.1017/rep.2022.30

Baumgartner, F., M. Davidson, K. R. Johnson, A. Krishnamurthy, & C. P. Wilson (2018). *Deadly Justice: A Statistical Portrait of the Death Penalty.* New York: Oxford University Press.

Baumgartner, F., & T. Lyman (2016). "Louisiana Death Sentenced Cases and Their Reversals, 1976–2015." *Journal of Race, Gender, and Poverty* 7, 58–75.

Baumgartner, F. R., & A. W. Dietrich (March 17, 2015). "Most Death Penalty Sentences Are Overturned. Here's Why That Matters." *The Washington Post*. https://www.washingtonpost.com/news/monkey-cage/wp/2015/03/17/most-death-penalty-sentences-are-overturned-heres-why-that-matters/

Baze v. Rees (2008). 553 U.S. 35.

Beccaria, C. (1764/1963). *On Crimes and Punishments*. Indianapolis, IN: Bobbs-Merrill.

Beck, E., S. Britto, & A. Andrews (2007). *In the Shadow of Death: Restorative Justice and Death Row Families*. New York: Oxford University Press.

Beckett, K., & H. Evans (2016). "Race, Death, and Justice: Capital Sentencing in Washington State, 1981–2014." *Columbia Journal of Race and Law* 6 (2), 77–114. https://doi.org/10.7916/cjrl.v6i2.2314.

Bedau, H. A. (1982). *The Death Penalty in America*. New York: Oxford University Press.

Bentele, U., & W. J. Bowers (2001). "How Jurors Decide on Death: Guilt Is Overwhelming; Aggravation Requires Death; and Mitigation Is No Excuse." *Brook Law Review* 66, 1011–1032.

Berkowitz, L., & J. Macaulay (1971). "The Contagion of Criminal Violence." *Sociometry* 34, 238–260.

Berns, N. (2009). "Contesting the Victim Card." *Sociological Quarterly* 50, 383–406.

Berns, W. (1979). *For Capital Punishment*. New York: Basic Books.

Bienen, L. B., N. A. Weiner, D. W. Denno, P. D. Allison, & D. L. Mills (1988). "The Reimposition of Capital Punishment in New Jersey: The Role of Prosecutorial Discretion." *Rutgers Law Review* 41, 27–172.

Black, C. L. (1974). *Capital Punishment: The Inevitability of Caprice and Mistake*. New York: Norton.

Blevins, K. R., & K. I. Minor (2018). "Race and the Death Penalty." In R. M. Bohm & G. Lee, eds., *Routledge Handbook on Capital Punishment*, 555–574. New York: Routledge.

Blume, J. H. (2010). "An Overview of Significant Findings from the Capital Jury Project and Other Empirical Studies of the Death Penalty Relevant to Jury Selection, Presentation of Evidence, and Jury Instructions in Capital Cases." https://secure.in.gov/ipdc/files/Overview-of-CJP-and-Other-Findings-spring-2010.pdf.

Bohm, R. M. (2013). *Capital Punishment's Collateral Damage*. Durham, NC: Carolina Academic Press.

Bohm, R. M. (2016). *Deathquest: An Introduction to the Theory and Practice of Capital Punishment in the United States*. New York: Taylor & Francis.

Bookman, M. (2021). *A Descending Spiral*. New York: New Press.

Booth v. Maryland (1987). 482 U.S. 496.

Borchard, E. (1932). *Convicting the Innocent*. New Haven, CT: Yale University Press.

Bosse v. Oklahoma (2016). 137 S. Ct. 1.

Bowers, W. J. (1974). *Executions in America*. Lexington, MA: Lexington Books.

Bowers, W. J. (1988). "The Effect of Executions is Brutalization, Not Deterrence." In K. C. Haas & J. A. Inciardi, eds., *Challenging Capital Punishment*, 49–89. Newbury Park, CA: Sage.

Bowers, W. J., B. Fleury-Steiner, & M. E. Antonio (2003). "The Capital Sentencing Decision: Guided Discretion, Reasoned Moral Judgment, or Legal fiction." In J. Acker, R. M. Bohm, & C. S. Lanier, eds., *America's Experiment with Capital Punishment*, 2nd ed., 413–468. Durham, NC: Carolina Academic Press.

Bowers, W. J., W. D. Foglia, S. Ehrhard-Dietzel, & C. E. Kelly (2010). "Jurors' Failure to Understand or Comport with Constitutional Standards in Capital Sentencing: Strength of the Evidence." *Criminal Law Bulletin* 46, 1147–1229.

Bowers, W. J., C. E. Kelly, R. Kleinstuber, E. S. Vartkessian, & M. Sandys (2014). "The Life or Death Sentencing Decision: It's at odds with Constitutional Standards; Is It Beyond Human Ability?" In J. R. Acker, R. M. Bohm, & C. S. Lanier, eds., *America's Experiment with Capital Punishment: Reflections on the Past, Present, and Future of the Ultimate Penal Sanction*, 3rd ed., 425–496. Durham, NC: Carolina Academic Press.

Bowers, W. J., & G. Pierce (1980). "Arbitrariness and Discrimination under Post-Furman Capital Statutes." *Crime and Delinquency* 26, 563–576.

Bowers, W. J., G. L. Pierce, & J. F. McDevitt (1984). *Legal Homicide*. Boston, MA: Northeastern University Press.

Brambila, N. (June 17, 2016). "Executing Justice: Pennsylvania's Death Penalty System Costs $816 Million." *The Reading Eagle*. https://www.readingeagle.com/ 2016/06/17/executing-justice-a-look-at-the-cost-of-pennsylvanias-death-penalty/

Brandon, C. (1999). *The Electric Chair: An Unnatural American History*. Jefferson, NC: McFarland.

Brenann, M. (June 9, 2022). *Americans Say Birth Control, Divorce Most "Morally Acceptable."* Gallup News.

Bright, S. B. & Kwak (2023). *The Fear of too much Justice*. New York, NY: The New Press.

Brook, T., J. Bourgon, & G. Blue (2008). *Death by a Thousand Cuts*. Cambridge, MA: Harvard University Press.

Brooks, J. (2023). *You Might Go to Prison, Even Though You're Innocent*. Berkeley: University of California Press.

Buck v. Davis (2017). 137 S. Ct. 759.

Burgason, K. A. (2018). "Capital Punishments Co-Victims." In R. M. Bohm & G. Lee, eds., *Routledge Handbook on Capital Punishment*, 612–630. New York: Routledge.

Butler, B. (2008). "The Role of Death Qualification in Venirepersons' Susceptibility to Victim Impact Statements." *Psychology, Crime & Law* 14 (2), 133–141.

Butler, L., J. D. Unnever, F. T. Cullen, & A. J. Thielo (2018). "Public Opinion About the Death Penalty." In R. M. Bohm & G. Lee, eds., *Routledge Handbook on Capital Punishment*, 55–70. New York: Routledge.

Cabana, D. A. (1998). *Death at Midnight*. Boston, MA: Northeastern University Press.

Caldwell v. Mississippi (1985). 472 U.S. 320.

Caldwell, N., A. Chang, & J. Myers (September 21, 2020). "Gasping for Air: Autopsies Reveal Troubling Effects of Lethal Injection." https://www.npr. org/2020/09/21/793177589/

California Commission on the Fair Administration of Justice (CCFAJ) (June 30, 2008). "Report and Recommendations on the Administration of the Death Penalty in California." http://death-penalty.org/downloads/FINAL%20REP ORT% 20DEATH%20 PENALTY%20ccfaj%20June%2030.2008.pdf

California Criminal Jury Instructions (CALCRIM) (2023). Homicide CALCRIM No. 763. Death Penalty: Factors to Consider – Not Identified as Aggravating or Mitigating (Pen. Code, § 190.3).

California v. Brown (1987). 479 U.S. 538.

Callins v. Collins (1994). 510 U.S. 1141.

Camus, A. (1960). *Reflections on the Guillotine.* New York: Penguin.

Capestany, G. (July 16, 2018). "Washington Voters Favor Death Penalty Alternatives." https://www.krem.com/article/news/politics/washington-voters-favor-death-penalty-alternatives/293-574445777

Chaney v. Heckler (1983). 718 F.2d.

Cline, A. (2017). *The Current War: A Battle Story Between Two Electrical Titans, Thomas Edison and George Westinghouse.* CreateSpace Independent Publishing Platform.

Cochran, J. K. (2018). "The Marshall Hypotheses." In R. M. Bohm & G. Lee, eds., *Handbook on Capital Punishment,* 71–85. London: Routledge.

Cohen, D. A. (1988). "In Defense of the Gallows." *American Quarterly* 40, 147–164.

Cohn, H. (1970). "The Penology of the Talmud." *Israel Law Review* 5, 451–463.

Collins, K. (February 6, 2019). "News Release: New Poll Shows Death Penalty Supporters Now in the Minority Among N.C. Voters." Center for Death Penalty Litigation. https://www.cdpl.org/new-poll-shows-death-penalty-supporters-now-in-the-minority-among-n-c-voters/

Collins, P. A., R. C. Boruchowitz, M. J. Hickman, & M. A. Larrañaga (2016). "An Analysis of the Economic Costs of Seeking the Death Penalty in Washington State." *Seattle Journal for Social Justice* 14 (3), 727–779. https://digitalcommons. law.seattleu. edu/sjsj/vol14/iss3/10

Collins, P. A., & A. Kaplan (October 28, 2019). "The Death Penalty Is Getting More and More Expensive. Is It Worth It?" The Conversation. https:// theconversation.com/the-death-penalty-is-getting-more-and-more-expens ive-is-it-worth-it-74294

Cook, P. J. (2009). "Potential Savings from Abolition of the Death Penalty in North Carolina, *American Law and Economics Review* 33, 1–32.

Cook, P. J., & D. Slawson (1993). *The Costs of Processing Murder Cases in North Carolina.* Durham, NC: Sanford School of Public Policy, Duke University Press.

Cooper, D. D. (1974). *The Lesson of the Scaffold.* Athens: Ohio University Press.

Costanzo, M., & S. Costanzo (1992). "Jury Decision Making in the Capital Penalty Phase: Legal Assumptions, Empirical Findings, and a Research Agenda." *Law and Human Behavior* 16, 185–202.

Costanzo, M., & S. Costanzo (1994). "The Death Penalty: Public Opinions, Legal Decisions, and Juror Perspectives." In M. Costanzo & S. Oskamp, eds., *Violence and the Law,* 246–271. Thousand Oaks, CA: Sage.

Costanzo, S., & M. Costanzo (1994). "Life or Death Decisions: An Analysis of Capital Jury Decision-Making Under the Special Issues Sentencing Framework." *Law and Human Behavior* 18, 151–170.

Costanzo, M., & J. Peterson (1994). "Attorney Persuasion in the Capital Penalty Phase: A Content Analysis of Closing Arguments." *Journal of Social Issues* 50, 125–148.

Cullen, F. T., J. D. Unnever, K. R. Blevins, J. A. Pealer, S. A. Santan, B. S. Fisher, & B. K. Applegate (2009). "The Myth of Public Support for the Death Penalty." In J. Wood & T. Gannon, eds., *Public Opinion and Criminal Justice*, 73–95. Cullompton, UK: Willan.

Cunningham, M. D. (2016). "Forensic Psychology Evaluations at Capital Sentencing." In R. Jackson & R. Roesch, eds., *Learning Forensic Assessment Research and Practice*, 202–228. New York: Routledge.

Curriden, M. (July 1995). "Hard Time." *ABA Journal* 70–75.

Cutler, J. E. (1907). *An Investigation into the History of Lynching in the United States.* New York: Longmans, Green, and Co.

Czachor, E. M. (January 26, 2024). "Kenneth Eugene Smith Executed by Nitrogen Hypoxia in Alabama, Marking a First for the Death Penalty. *CBS News.* https:// www.cbsnews.com/news/kenneth-eugene-smith-executed-by-nitrogen-hypoxia-in-alabama/

Dann, R. H. (1935). *The Deterrent Effect of Capital Punishment.* Philadelphia, PA: Central Bureau of Philadelphia Yearly Meeting of Friends

Date, S. V. (January 4, 2000). "The High Price of Killing Killers." *The Palm Beach Post*, 1A.

Death Penalty Information Center (DPIC) (2002). "Misconduct Reversals and Exonerations." https://deathpenaltyinfo.org/policy-issues/prosecutorial-account ability/misconduct-reversals-and-exonerations-by-type

Death Penalty Information Center (DPIC) (2023). "Fact Sheet." https://dpic-cdn. org/ production/documents/pdf/FactSheet.pdf

Death Penalty Information Center (DPIC) (2023). "Doomed to Repeat: The Legacy of Race in Tennessee's Contemporary Death Penalty." https://dpic-cdn.org/pro duction/documents/pdf/ DPIC-Tenessee-Report-Doomed-to-Repeat_2023-06-23-134404_zsfd.pdf?dm1687527844

Death Penalty Information Center (DPIC) (2024). *Innocence.* https://deathpenaltyi nfo.org/policy-issues/innocences

Denno, D. W. (2007). "The Lethal Injection Quandary: How Medicine Has Dismantled the Death Penalty." *Fordham Law Review* 76, 49–128.

Denno, D. W. (2018). "Execution Methods in a Nutshell." In R. M. Bohm & G. Lee, eds., *Routledge Handbook on Capital Punishment*, 427–446. New York: Routledge.

Diaz, J. (May 12, 2022). "U.S. Inmates Condemned to Die Are Spending More Time on Death Row." National Public Radio. https://www.npr.org/2022/05/12/109 7184110/death-row-inmates-execution-time

Donohue, J. J., & J. Wolfers (2006). "The Death Penalty: No Evidence for Deterrence." *Economists' Voice* 4, 1–6.

Donohue, J. J., & J. Wolfers (2010). "Uses and Abuses of Empirical Evidence in the Death Penalty Debate." *Stanford Law Review* 58, 791–846.

Duff, C. (1961). *A Handbook on Hanging: Being a Short Introduction to the Fine Art of Execution*. London: Putnam.

Eagleman, D. (2011). *Incognito: The Secret Life of the Brain*. New York: Vintage.

Eddings v. Oklahoma (1982). L. Ed. 2d 1, at 71.

Ehrlich, I. (1975). "The Deterrent Effect of Capital Punishment: A Question of Life and Death." *American Economic Review* 65, 397–417.

Ellsworth, P. C., & S. R. Gross (1994). "Hardening of the Attitudes: Americans' Views on the Death Penalty." *Journal of Social Issues* 50, 19–52.

Evans, E. P. (1906). *The Criminal Prosecution and Capital Punishment of Animals*. London: Heinemann.

Fagan, J., F. Zimring, & A. Geller (2006). "Capital Punishment and Capital Murder: Market Share and the Deterrent Effects of the Death Penalty." *Texas Law Review* 84, 1803. https://scholarship.law.columbia.edu/faculty_scholarship/1424

Feldman, P. (April 6, 1995). "The Mundane Murder Trial Down the Hall." *Los Angeles Times*, A20.

Fink, D. S., J. Santaella-Tenorio, & K. M. Keyes (2018). "Increase in Suicides the Months After the Death of Robin Williams in the US." *PLoS ONE* 13 (2), e0191405. https://doi.org/10.1371/journal.pone.0191405

Fleury-Steiner, B. (2007). *Jurors' Stories of Death: How America's Death Penalty Invests in Inequality*. Ann Arbor: University of Michigan Press.

Flowers v. Mississippi (2019). 139 S. Ct. 2228.

Foglia, W. D., & M. Sandys (2018). "The Capital Jury and Sentencing: Neither Guided Nor Individualized." In R. M. Bohm & G. Lee, eds., *Routledge Handbook on Capital Punishment*, 364–384. New York: Routledge.

Forsberg, M. E. (November 2005). "Money for Nothing: The Financial Cost of New Jersey's Death Penalty." New Jersey Policy Perspective. www.njadp.org/forms/cost/MoneyforNothing November18.html

Frank, J., & B. Frank (1957). *Not Guilty*. Garden City, NY: Doubleday.

Freinkel, A., C. Koopman, & D. Spiegel (1994). "Dissociative Symptoms in Media Eyewitnesses of an Execution." *American Journal of Psychiatry* 151, 1335–1339.

Furman v. Georgia (1972). 408 U.S. 238.

Gallup (2022). Historical Trends: The Death Penalty. https://news.gallup.com /poll/1606/death-penalty.aspx

Garrett, B. L. (2017). *End of Its Rope*. Cambridge, MA: Harvard University Press.

Gazzaniga, M. (2011). *Who's in Charge?: Free Will and the Science of the Brain*. New York: Harper-Collins.

Gilmore, M. (1994). *Shot in the Heart*. New York: Doubleday.

Glossip v. Gross (2015). 135 S. Ct. 2726.

Goldfarb, P. (2016). "Matters of Strata: Race, Gender, and Class Structures in Capital Cases." *Washington & Lee Law Review* 73, 386–424. https://scholarlycommons.law.wlu.edu/wlulr/vol73/iss3/11.

Gramlich, J. (October 31, 2022). "Violent Crime Is a Key Midterm Voting Issue, but What Does the Data Say?" Pew Research Center. https://pewrsr.ch/3Wleags

Greenblatt, I. (August 21, 2020). "He Deserves Nothing: More Survivors of Joseph DeAngelo's Brutal Crimes to Testify Wednesday." ABC News 10, Sacramento. https://www.abc10.com/article/news/crime/more-survivors-of-joseph-deangelos-brutal-crimes-to-testify-wednesday/103-69b008c4-4160-415c-8cd8-303949dc035d

Gregg v. Georgia (1976). 428 U.S. 153.

Griffin, V. W., & O. H. Griffin (2018). "The Appellate Process in Capital Cases." In R. M. Bohm & G. Lee, eds. *Routledge Handbook on Capital Punishment*, 399–410. New York: Routledge.

Gross, S. R., & R. Mauro (1989). *Death and Discrimination: Racial Disparities in Capital Sentencing*. Boston: Northeastern University Press.

Gross, S. R., B. O'Brien, B., C. Hu, & E. H. Kennedy (2014). "Rate of False Conviction of Criminal Defendants Who Are Sentenced to Death." *PNAS Proceedings of the National Academy of Sciences of the United States of America* 111 (20), 7230–7235. https://doi.org/10.1073/pnas.1306417111

Hamilton, L., ed. (1854). *Memoirs, Speeches and Writings of Robert Rantoul Jr.* Boston: John P. Jewett.

Haney, C. (2005). *Death by Design*. New York: Oxford University Press.

Haney, C., L. Sontag, & S. Costanzo (1994). "Deciding to Take a Life." *Journal of Social Issues* 50, 149–176.

Haney, C., E. L. Zurbriggen, & J. M. Weill (2022). "The Continuing Unfairness of Death Qualification: Changing Death Penalty Attitudes and Capital Jury Selection." *Psychology, Public Policy, and Law* 28, 1–31. https://doi.org/10.1037/law0000335

Hanson, C. (October 31, 1995). "Few of Those Accused Get Dream Team." *Los Angeles Daily Journal*, 21–24.

Harmon, T., & D. L. Falco (2018). "Wrongful Capital Convictions." In R. Bohm & G. Lee, eds., *Routledge Handbook on Capital Punishment*, 575–588. New York: Routledge.

Harmon, T. R., D. L. Falco, & D. Taylor (2022). "The Impact of Specific Knowledge on Death Penalty Opposition: An Empirical Test of the Marshall Hypothesis." *Crime & Delinquency* 68 (9), 1516–1537. https://doi.org/10.1177/0011128721 1052441

Harmon, T. R., D. Taylor, & C. Henning (2023). "A Reflection on Contemporary Issues Regarding the Death Penalty." *Journal of Criminal Justice and Law*. https://jcjl.pubpub.org/pub/1y6bwlz8

Harris, S. (2012). *Free Will*. New York: Free Press.

Henry, T. A. (August 22, 2018). "AMA to Supreme Court: Doctor Participation in Executions Unethical." https://www.ama-assn.org/delivering-care/ethics/ama-supreme-court-doctor-participation-executions-unethical

Hillman, H. (1993). "The Possible Pain Experienced During Execution by Different Methods." *Perception* 22, 745–753.

Holloway, J. F. (2021). "Instilling a Culture of Continuous Learning from Criminal Justice Systems Errors: A Multi-Stakeholder Sentinel Event Review Process in

Philadelphia." Office of Justice Programs: National Institute of Justice. https://www.ojp.gov/pdffiles1/nij/grants/256006.pdf

Hood, R., & C. Hoyle (2009). "Abolishing the Death Penalty Worldwide: The Impact of a 'New Dynamic.'" *Crime and Justice* 38 (1), 1–63. https://doi.org/10.1086/599200

Hook, D. D., & L. Kahn (1989). *Death in the Balance*. Lexington, MA: D. C. Heath.

Hoppe, C. (March 8, 1992). "Executions Cost Texas Millions." *The Dallas Morning News*, A4.

Horwitz, E. L. (1973). *Capital Punishment, USA*. Philadelphia: Lippincott Co.

Huesmann, L. (2018). "The Contagion of Violence." In A. Vazsonyi, D. Flannery, & M. DeLisi, eds., *The Cambridge Handbook of Violent Behavior and Aggression*, 527–556. Cambridge: Cambridge University Press. https://doi.org/10.1017/9781316847992.030

Hurst v. Florida (2016). 577 U.S. 92.

Innocence Project (2023). "The Causes of Wrongful Convictions." https://innocenceproject.org/

Innocence Project (2023). "Transforming Systems." https://innocenceproject.org/transforming-systems/

In re: Ohio Execution Protocol Litigation (January 14, 2019). No. 11-cv-1016, 2019 WL 244488, at 70 (S.D. Ohio January 14, 2019).

Johnson, R. (2005). *Death Work: A Study of the Modern Execution Process*. Pacific Grove, CA: Brooks/Cole.

Johnson, R. (2018). "Living and Working on Death Row." In R. M. Bohm & G. Lee, eds., *Routledge Handbook on Capital Punishment*, 589–594. New York: Routledge.

Johnson, R. (2019). *Condemned to Die: Life Under the Sentence of Death*. New York: Routledge.

Johnson, R., & A. Dobrzanska (2005). "Mature Coping Among Life-Sentenced Inmates: An Exploratory Study of Adjustment Dynamics." *Corrections Compendium* 27, 8–14.

Jones, E. (2020). "The Inherent Implicit Racism in Capital Crime Jury Deliberation." *Virginia Journal of Criminal Law*, 109, 110–127.

Judicial Council, Kansas Legislature. (February 13, 2014). "Report of the Judicial Council Death Penalty Advisory Committee.", 1–36. https://www.aclu.org/wp-content/uploads/legal-documents/2022.03.04_-_report_on_cost_final.pdf

Justice Research Group (February 17, 2022). "The Modern American Death Penalty Is Massively Unpopular." https://docs.google.com/document/d/1dy5tjZwoK4sknYIayiYZnE6xvIdHUew30GfXLNFejM8/edit

Kane, K. (1986). "Forgotten Families of Death Row." *The Defender*, 33–35.

Kant, I. (1797/1965). *The Metaphysical Elements of Justice*. Indianapolis: Bobbs-Merrill.

Kaplan, A. B., P. A. Collins, & V. L. Mayhew (2016). *Oregon's Death Penalty: A Cost Analysis*. Seattle, WA: Lewis & Clark Law School and Seattle University.

Kaufman, S. B. (2020). *American Roulette*. Berkeley: University of California Press.

King, D. R. (1979). "The Brutalization Effect." *Social Forces* 57, 683–687.

King, K. (2004). "It Hurts So Bad: Comparing Grieving Patterns of the Families of Murder Victims with Those of Families of Death Row Inmates." *Criminal Justice Policy Review* 15 (2), 193–211.

King, G. (2009). *The Execution of Willie Francis: Race, Murder, and the Search for Justice in the American South*. New York: Basic Books.

King James Bible (1769/2017). "King James Bible Online." https://www.kingjames bibleonline.org/

Klein, L. R., B. E. Forst, & V. Filatov (1978). "The Deterrent Effect of Capital Punishment: An Assessment of the Estimates." In A. Blumstein, J. Cohen, & D. Nagin, eds., *Deterrence and Incapacitation*. Washington DC: National Academy of Sciences.

Koch, C. (2012). "Finding free will." *Scientific American* 23 (2), 22–27. http://dx.doi.org/10.1038/scientificamericanmind0512-22

Koestler, A. (1957). *Reflections on Hanging*. New York: Macmillan.

Kovandzic, T. V., L. M. Vieraitis, & D. P. Boots (2009). "Does the Death Penalty Save Lives?" *Criminology & Public Policy* 8, 803–843. https://doi.org/10.1111/j.1745-9133.2009.00596.x

Kruse, K. R. (2015). "Wrongful Convictions and Upstream Reform in the Criminal Justice System." *Texas A&M Law Review* 367. https://doi.org/10.37419/LR.V3.I2.5

Larranga, M. A., & D. Mustard (2004). "Washington's Death Penalty System: A Review of the Costs, Length, and Results of Capital Cases in Washington State. Washington Death Penalty Assistance Center. http://abolishdeathpenalty.org/wp-content/uploads/2013/08/ WAStateDeathPenaltyCosts.pdf

Latzer, B., & J. N. G. Cauthen (2007). "Justice Delayed? Time Consumption in Capital Appeals: A Multistate Study." Research report submitted to the U.S. Department of Justice. https://www.ojp.gov/pdffiles1/nij/grants/217555.pdf

Laurence, J. (1931). *A History of Capital Punishment*. London: Sampson, Low, Marston.

Leahy, M., R. Blecker, W. M. Erlbaum, J. Fagan, N. Greene, J. Kirchmeier, & D. Von Drehle (2003). "Rethinking the Death Penalty: Can We Define Who Deserves Death? *Pace Law Review* 24 (1), 107–186.

Legislative Services Agency (January 6, 2010). "Murder Sentencing and Sentence Enhancement, Fiscal Impact Statement." http://www.in.gov/legislative Indiana Office of Fiscal and management Analysis. www.deathpenaltyinfo.org/docume nts/INCostAssess.pdf

Lempert, R. O. (1983). "The Effect of Executions on Homicides: A New Look in an Old Light." *Crime and Delinquency* 29, 88–115.

Levinson, J.D., R.J. Smith, & D.M. Young (2014). "Devaluing Death: An Empirical Study of Implicit Racial Bias on Jury-Eligible Citizens in Six Death Penalty States." *New York University Law Review* 89 (2), 513–581. https://www.nyulawreview.org/wp-content/uploads/2018/08/NYULawReview-89-2-LevinsonSmithYoung.pdf.

Liebman, J. S., J. Fagan, & V. West (2000). "A Broken System: Error Rates in Capital Cases." *Texas Law Review* 78, 1839–1861.

Lifton, R.J., & G. Mitchell (2002). *Who Owns Death?: Capital Punishment, the American Conscience, and the End of Executions*. New York: Harper Collins.

Locke, J. (1690/1963). *Two Treatises of Government*. Cambridge: Cambridge University Press.

Lockett v. Ohio (1978). 438 U.S. 586.

Lyman, T., F. R. Baumgartner, & G. L. Pierce (2022). "Race and Gender Disparities in Capitally-Charged Louisiana Homicide Cases, 1976–2014." *CrimRxiv*. https://doi.org/10.21428/cb6ab371.e2dbcb75

Lynch, M., & C. Haney (2009). "Capital Jury Deliberation: Effects on Death Sentencing, Comprehension, and Discrimination." *Law and Human Behavior* 33 (6), 481.

Malinowski, B. (1954). *Magic, Science and Religion and Other Essays*. Garden City, NY: Doubleday.

Mandery, E. J. (2013). *A Wild Justice*. New York: Norton.

Manski, C. F., & J. V. Pepper (2013). "Deterrence and the Death Penalty: Partial Identification Analysis Using Repeated Cross Sections." *Journal of Quantitative Criminology* 29, 123–141. https://doi.org/10.1007/s10940-012-9172-z

McCleskey v. Kemp (1987). 481 U.S. 279.

McCord, D., & T. R. Harmon (2018). "Lethal Rejection: An Empirical Analysis of the Astonishing Plunge in Death Sentences in the United States from Their Post-Furman Peak." *Albany Law Review* 81, 201–218.

McFarland, T. (2016). "The Death Penalty vs. Life Incarceration: A Financial Analysis." *Susquehanna University Political Review* 7, 46–614. https://scholarly commons.susqu.edu/supr/vol7/iss1/

McGautha v. California (1971). 402 U.S. 183.

Miller, M. K., & R. Hayward (2008). "Religious Characteristics and the Death Penalty." *Law and Human Behavior* 32, 113–123.

Mitchell, K., B. Myers, & N. Broszkiewicz (2015). "Good or Essential? The Effects of Victim Characteristics and Family Significance on Sentencing Judgments and Perceptions of Harm." *Psychiatry, Psychology and Law* 23, 631–669.

Morganthau, T. (August 7, 1995). "Condemned to Life." *Newsweek*, 19–23.

Morris, P. (2021). "Sentenced to Death but Innocent." *National Geographic*. https://www.nationalgeographic.com/history/article/sentenced-to-death-but-innocent-these-are-stories-of-justice-gone-wrong

Morrison v. State (2002). 71 S.W.3d 821 (Tex. App. 2002).

Myers, B., N. Nuñez, B. Wilkowski, A. Kehn, & K. Dunn (2018). "The Heterogeneity of Victim Impact Statements: A Content Analysis of Capital Trial Sentencing Penalty Phase Transcripts." *Psychology, Public Policy, and Law* 24, 474–488. http://dx.doi.org/10.1037/law0000185

Nakell, B. (1987). "The cost of the death penalty." In H.A. Bedau, ed., *The Death Penalty in America*, 241–246. Philadelphia, PA.

Nathanson, S. (1987). *An Eye for an Eye?* Totowa, NJ: Rowman & Littlefield.

National Registry of Exonerations (NRE) (2023). John Huffington. https://www.law.umich.edu special/exoneration/Pages/ casedetail. aspx?caseid6541

National Research Council (NRC) (2012). *Deterrence and the Death Penalty.* Washington, DC: National Academies Press. https://doi.org/10.17226/13363.

Nestor, P. G. (2019). "In Defense of Free Will: Neuroscience and Criminal Responsibility." *Journal of Law and Psychiatry* 65, Article ID: 101344.

Newsweek. (July 28, 1995). "Killing Me Cruelly?" www.newsweek.com

Pappas, S. (2015). "In Boston and Aurora, Jurors May Risk Mental Health for Justice." *Live Science.* https://www.livescience.com/49607-boston-aurora-jury-selection-mental-health.html

Paley, W. (1790). *Commentaries on the Laws of England* 4. Worcester, MA: Thomas.

Paternoster, R. (1991). *Capital Punishment in America.* New York: Lexington Books.

Paternoster, R., & R. Brame (2008). "Reassessing Race Disparities in Maryland Capital Cases." *Criminology* 46, 971–1008.

Paternoster, R., & J. Deise (2011). "A Heavy Thumb on the Scale: The Effect of Victim Impact Evidence on Capital Decision Making." *Criminology* 49, 129–161.

Paternoster, R., & A. Kazyaka (1988). "Administration of the Death Penalty in South Carolina: Experiences Over the First Few Years." *South Carolina Law Review* 39, 245–414.

Payne v. Tennessee (1991). 111 S. Ct. 2597.

Payton, R. (March 6, 1997). "How Parents of Slain Children Cope." *Oakland Tribune*, C7.

Pazzani, L. (2018). "Capital Punishment and Victims' and Offenders' Families." In R. M. Bohm & G. Lee, eds., *Routledge Handbook on Capital Punishment*, 595–611. New York: Routledge.

Peiser, J., & C. Armario (October 29, 2021). "Oklahoma Death Row Inmate Convulsed, Vomited During Lethal Injection, Witness Says, As State Resumes Executions." *Washington Post.* https://www.washingtonpost.com/national/oklahoma-resumes-executions-inmate-put-to-death-for-1998-slaying/2021/10/28/0871af4c-33aa-11ec-a1e5-07223c50280a_story.html

Petersen, N. (2017). "Examining the Sources of Racial Bias in Potentially Capital Cases: A Case Study of Police and Prosecutorial Discretion." *Race and Justice* 7 (1), 7–34.

Peterson, R. D., & W. C. Bailey (1988). "Murder and Capital Punishment in the Evolving Context of the Post-Furman Era." *Social Forces* 66, 774–807.

Pilkington, E. (March 29, 2017). "Eight Executions in 11 days: Arkansas Order May Endanger Staff's Mental Health." *The Guardian.* https://www.theguardian.com/world/2017/mar/29/arkansas-executioners-mental-health-allen-ault.

Pilkington, E. (December 28, 2022). "What Is It Like to Survive an Execution by Lethal Injection?" *The Guardian.* https://www.theguardian.com/world/2022/dec/28/lethal-injection-surviving-execution-attempt-alabama

Pilkington, E. (January 26, 2024). "Alabama Inmate Executed with Nitrogen Gas Was 'Shaking Violently', Witnesses Say." *The Guardian.* https://www.theguardian.com/us-news/2024/jan/25/alabama-executes-kenneth-smith-nitrogen-gas

Pitt, D. (2013). "No Payne, No Gain? Revisiting Victim Impact Statements After Twenty Years in Effect." *Chapman Law Review* 16, 475–499.

Pope John Paul II (1995). *The Gospel of Life: On the Value and Inviolability of Human Life*. Washington, DC: United States Catholic Conference.

Porter, J. R., E. Morrison, S. Chintakrindi, & D. Shapley (2018). "The Historically Enduring Gap in Death Penalty Support: Re-Examining the Role of Context in the Recent History of the Black-White Divide." *Kriminologija & socijalna integracija: časopis za kriminologiju, penologiju i poremećaje u ponašanju*, 26 (2), 136–159.

Prescott, J. J., B. Pyle, & S. B. Starr (2020). "Understanding Violent-Crime Recidivism." *Notre Dame Law Review* 95 (4), 1643–1698.

Primus, E. B. (2020). "Disaggregating Ineffective Assistance of Counsel Doctrine: Four Forms of Constitutional Ineffectiveness." *Stanford Law Review* 72, 1581–1653.

Public Policy Polling (2017). Utah Survey Results. information@publicpolicypolling.com

Radelet, M.L. (1989). "Executions of Whites for Crimes Against Blacks: Exceptions to the Rule." *Sociological Quarterly* 30 (4), 529–544. https://doi.org/10.1111/j.1533-8525.1989.tb01533.x.

Radelet, M. L. (2017). *The History of the Death Penalty in Colorado*. Boulder: University Press of Colorado. http://www.jstor.org/stable/j.ctt1k85dkv

Rancourt, M. A., C. Ouellet, & Y. Dufresne (2020). "Is the Death Penalty Debate Really Dead? Contrasting Capital Punishment Support in Canada and the United States." *Analyses of Social Issues and Public Policy* 20 (1), 536–562.

Reiman, J. (1988). "The Justice of the Death Penalty in an Unjust World." In K. C. Haas & J. A. Inciardi, eds., *Challenging Capital Punishment*, 29–48. Newbury Park, CA: Sage.

Reiman, J., & P. Leighton (2023). *The Rich Get Richer and the Poor Get Prison*. New York: Routledge.

Ring v. Arizona (2002). 536 U.S. 584.

Roberts v. Louisiana (1976). 428 U.S. 325.

Roman, J., A. Chalfin, A. Sundquiest, C. Knight, & A. Darmenov (2008). "The Cost of the Death Penalty." Urban Institute, Justice Policy Center. https://www.urban.org/research/publication/costs-death-penalty

Roper v. Simmons (2005). 543 U.S. 551.

Royal Commission on Capital Punishment (1953). "Evidence and papers." London: The National Archives. https://discovery.nationalarchives.gov.uk/details/r/C9165

Sahagun, L. (January 22, 1996). "Utah Is Under Fire Over Firing Squads." *Los Angeles Times*, A1.

Schneider, V., & J. Smykla (1991). "A Summary Analysis of Executions in the United States, 1608–1987: The Espy File." In R. Bohm, ed., *The Death Penalty in America: Current Perspectives*, 1–19. Cincinnati, OH: Anderson.

Scott, G. R. (1950). *The History of Capital Punishment*. London: Torchstream Books.

Sellin, T. (1980). *The Penalty of Death*. Beverly Hills, CA: Sage.

Shaked-Schroer, N., M. Costanzo, & A. Marcus-Newhall (2008). "Reducing Racial Bias in the Penalty Phase of Capital Trials." *Behavioral Sciences & the Law* 26 (5), 603–617.

Sharp, S. F. (2005). *Hidden Victims: The Effect of the Death Penalty on the Families of the Accused*. New Brunswick, NJ: Rutgers University Press.

Shepherd, J. M. (2005). "Deterrence Versus Brutalization: Capital Punishment's Differing Impacts Among States." *Michigan Law Review* 104 (2), 203–256.

Sheppard, S. R. (1995). "In the Belly of the Death Penalty Beast." In *The Machinery of Death*, 59–73. New York: Amnesty International USA.

Skipper v. South Carolina (1986). 476 U.S. 1.

Smith, D. G. (September 23, 2022). "New Execution Method Touted as More 'Humane,' but Evidence Is Lacking." *Scientific American*. https://www.scientifica merican.com/article/new-execution-method-touted-as-more-humane-but-evide nce-is-lacking/

Smith, R. J. (2012). "The Geography of the Death Penalty and Its Ramifications." *Boston University Law Review* 92, 227–289.

Songer, M. J., & I. Unah (2006). "The Effect of Race, Gender, and Location on Prosecutorial Decisions to Seek the Death Penalty." *South Carolina Law Review* 58, 161–210.

Sorensen, J. R., & T. J. Reidy (2019). "Nothing to Lose? An Examination of Prison Misconduct Among Life-Without-Parole Inmates." *Prison Journal* 99 (1), 46–65. https://doi.org/10.1177/0032885518814719

Statistica Research (June 2, 2023). "Reported Violent Crime Rate in the U.S. 1980–2021." www.statista.com/statistics/191219/reported-viol ent-crime-rate-in-the-usa-since-1980/

Steiker, C. C., & J. M. Steiker (2015). "The American Death Penalty and the (In) Visibility of Race." *University of Chicago Law Review* 82 (1) 243–294.

Sullivan, J. (January 7, 2015). "Seeking Death Penalty Adds $1M to Prosecution Cost, Study Says." *Seattle Times*. https://timothyburgess.typepad.com/files/2015-01-26-death-penalty-letter.pdf

Sundby, S. E. (2010). "War and Peace in the Jury Room: How Capital Juries Reach Unanimity." *Hastings Law Journal* 103, 107–111.

Swafford, A. T. (2011). "Qualified Support: Death Qualification, Equal Protection, and Race." *American Journal of Criminal Law* 39, 147–158.

Szmania, S. J., & M. L. Gracyalny (2006). "Addressing the Court, the Offender, and the Community: A Communication Analysis of Victim Impact Statements." *International Review of Victimology* 13, 231–249.

Tabak, R. (2022). "Capital Punishment: The State of Criminal Justice 2023." American Bar Association Criminal Justice Section. https://www.americanbar.org/content/dam/aba/publications/criminaljustice/2023/death-penalty-scj2023.pdf

Tabak, R. J., & M. Lane (1989). "The Execution of Justice: A Cost and Lack-of-Benefit Analysis of the Death Penalty." *Loyola of Los Angeles Law Review* 23 (2), 59–146.

Thomas, T. (2000). "Execution Impact Evidence in Kentucky: It Is Time to Return the Scales to Balance." *Northern Kentucky Law Review* 27, 411–429.

Thompson v. Oklahoma (1988). 487 U.S. 815.

Timmins, A. (2010). "Former Warden 'Haunted' by Executions, Death Penalty Scars Prison Staff, He Says." *Concord Monitor*. https://deathpenaltyinfo.org/new-voi ces-former-warden-calls-executions-traumatic-prison-staff

Trahan, A., K. Laird, & D. Evans (2018). "The Topography of Capital Punishment: Geographic Variations in Seeking, Achieving, and Carrying out the Death Penalty." In R. M. Bohm & G. Lee, eds., *Routledge Handbook on Capital Punishment*. New York: Routledge.

Trombley, S. (1992). *The Execution Protocol: Inside America's Capital Punishment Industry*. New York: Crown.

United Methodist Church (2016). Book of Discipline. https://www.ctcumc.org/files/fileshare/2016-book-of-discipline.pdf

Van den Haag, E., & J. Conrad (1983). *The Death Penalty: A Debate*. New York: Plenum.

Vandiver, M. (2018). "The Impact of the Death Penalty on Families of Homicide Victims and Condemned Prisoners." In J. R. Acker, R. M. Bohm, & C. S. Lanier, eds., *America's Experiment with Capital Punishment*, 627–660. Durham, NC: Carolina Academic Press.

Vito, G. F., & A. G. Vito (2017). "General Deterrence and Brutalization." In R. M. Bohm, & G. M. Lee, eds., *Routledge Handbook on Capital Punishment*, 170–182. New York: Routledge.

Von Drehle, D. (1995). *Among the Lowest of the Dead*. New York: Times Books.

Wainwright v. Witt (1985). 105 S. Ct. 844.

Wallace, A. (April 22, 1992). "Relatives of Two Victims Weigh Emotional Toll." *Los Angeles Times*. https://www.latimes.com/archives/la-xpm-1992-04-22-mn-535-story.html

Weeks v. *Angelone* (2000). 528 US 225.

Wegner, Daniel (2002). *The Illusion of Conscious Will*. Cambridge, MA: MIT Press.

Weisberg, R. (1994). "Deregulating Death." In P. Kurland, G. Casper, & D. Hutchinson, eds., *The Supreme Court Review*, 305–395. Chicago: University of Chicago Press.

Westervelt, S. D., & E. J. Cook (2012). *Life After Death Row: Exoneree's Search for Community and Identity*. New Brunswick, NJ: Rutgers University Press.

Williams, L. M. (July 2001). "Case Study on State and County Costs Associated with Capital Adjudication in Arizona: Data Set III Research Report to Arizona Capital Case Commission. The Williams Institute. www.azag.gov/sites/default /fi les/sites/all/docs/Criminal/ ccc/Attachment%20D%20-%20Data%20Set%20III.pdf

Wills, D. (2019). *Killing Times: The Temporal Technology of the Death Penalty, at 87*. New York: Fordham University Press.

Wolff, K. T., & M. K. Miller (2009). "Victim and Execution Impact Statements: What Judges Should Know About Case Law and Psychological Research." *Judicature* 92, 148–157.

Wolfgang, M., & M. Riedel (1973). "Race, Judicial Discretion, and the Death Penalty." *Annals of the American Academy of Political and Social Science* 407, 119–133.

Woodson v. North Carolina (1976). 428 U.S. 280.

Woodward, B., & S. Armstrong (1979). *The Brethren: Inside the Supreme Court*. New York: Avon.

Wooldredge, J. (2020). "Prison Culture, Management, and In-Prison Violence." *Annual Review of Criminology* 3 (1), 165–188.

Yang, B., & D. Lester (2008). "The Deterrent Effect of Executions A Meta-Analysis Thirty Years After Ehrlich." *Journal of Criminal Justice* 36, 453–460.

Yelderman, L. A., M. K. Miller, & C. D. Peoples (2016). "Capital-izing Jurors: How Death Qualification Relates to Jury Composition, Jurors' Perceptions, and Trial Outcomes." In B. H. Bornstein & M. K. Miller, eds., *Advances in Psychology and Law*, vol. 2, 27–54. New York: Springer.

Zimring, F. E., & G. Hawkins (1986). *Capital Punishment and the American Agenda.* Cambridge: Cambridge University Press.

Zivot, J. B., M. A. Edgar, & D. A. Lubarshy (2022). "Execution by Lethal Injection: Autopsy Findings of Pulmonary Edema." *MedRxiv.* https://doi.org/10.1101/2022. 08.24.22279183

For the benefit of digital users, indexed terms that span two pages (e.g., 52–53) may, on occasion, appear on only one of those pages.

www.ingramcontent.com/pod-product-compliance
Lightning Source LLC
Chambersburg PA
CBHW071223100426
42868CB00034B/499